CAMBRIDGE LIBRARY COLLECTION

Books of enduring scholarly value

Cambridge

The city of Cambridge received its royal charter in 1201, having already been home to Britons, Romans and Anglo-Saxons for many centuries. Cambridge University was founded soon afterwards and celebrated its octocentenary in 2009. This series explores the history and influence of Cambridge as a centre of science, learning, and discovery, its contributions to national and global politics and culture, and its inevitable controversies and scandals.

Gradus ad Cantabrigiam

This anonymous and light-hearted work was first published in 1803: reissued here is the edition of 1824, of which the authors describe themselves as 'a Brace of Cantabs'. It claims both to be a guide to 'the academical customs' of the university and to its 'colloquial or cant terms' with notes on those that differ from the usage of Oxford. The balance of information is given to the less serious aspects of university life: for example, considerably more space is given, in the definition of 'bishop', to a recipe for mulled port wine than to the clerical role. The work abounds in puns (in English and Latin), anecdotes, and extracts (mostly amusing) from more serious histories of the university, and ends with a tailpiece on how to graduate 'the reading way' and 'the varmint way'. This fascinating work demonstrates that the publication of spoof 'guides to freshmen' is nothing new.

Cambridge University Press has long been a pioneer in the reissuing of out-of-print titles from its own backlist, producing digital reprints of books that are still sought after by scholars and students but could not be reprinted economically using traditional technology. The Cambridge Library Collection extends this activity to a wider range of books which are still of importance to researchers and professionals, either for the source material they contain, or as landmarks in the history of their academic discipline.

Drawing from the world-renowned collections in the Cambridge University Library and other partner libraries, and guided by the advice of experts in each subject area, Cambridge University Press is using state-of-the-art scanning machines in its own Printing House to capture the content of each book selected for inclusion. The files are processed to give a consistently clear, crisp image, and the books finished to the high quality standard for which the Press is recognised around the world. The latest print-on-demand technology ensures that the books will remain available indefinitely, and that orders for single or multiple copies can quickly be supplied.

The Cambridge Library Collection brings back to life books of enduring scholarly value (including out-of-copyright works originally issued by other publishers) across a wide range of disciplines in the humanities and social sciences and in science and technology.

Gradus ad Cantabrigiam

*Or, New University Guide to the Academical Customs,
and Colloquial or Cant Terms
Peculiar to the University of Cambridge,
Observing Wherein It Differs from Oxford*

ANONYMOUS

CAMBRIDGE
UNIVERSITY PRESS

CAMBRIDGE
UNIVERSITY PRESS

University Printing House, Cambridge, CB2 8BS, United Kingdom

Cambridge University Press is part of the University of Cambridge.
It furthers the University's mission by disseminating knowledge in the pursuit of
education, learning and research at the highest international levels of excellence.

www.cambridge.org
Information on this title: www.cambridge.org/9781108078764

© in this compilation Cambridge University Press 2015

This edition first published 1824
This digitally printed version 2015

ISBN 978-1-108-07876-4 Paperback

GRADUS

AD

CANTABRIGIAM;

OR, THE

NEW UNIVERSITY GUIDE.

"Post tot naufragia, tutus" sum
Baccalaureus Artium.

GRADUS

AD

CANTABRIGIAM;

OR

NEW UNIVERSITY GUIDE TO THE ACADEMICAL CUSTOMS, AND
COLLOQUIAL OR CANT TERMS PECULIAR TO

𝕿𝖍𝖊 𝖀𝖓𝖎𝖛𝖊𝖗𝖘𝖎𝖙𝖞 𝖔𝖋 𝕮𝖆𝖒𝖇𝖗𝖎𝖉𝖌𝖊;

OBSERVING WHEREIN IT DIFFERS FROM OXFORD.

EMBELLISHED WITH SIX COLOURED ENGRAVINGS OF THE COSTUME, &c.
A STRIKING LIKENESS OF THAT CELEBRATED CHARACTER *JEMMY GORDON,* AND
ILLUSTRATED WITH A VARIETY OF CURIOUS AND ENTERTAINING ANECDOTES:

TO WHICH IS AFFIXED,

A TAIL-PIECE;

OR, THE READING AND VARMINT METHOD OF PROCEEDING
TO THE DEGREE OF A.B.

BY A BRACE OF CANTABS.

——————— ΚΗΜΟΣ ΚΑΛΟΣ !!!
Aristoph. Vespæ. 99.
Live for ever my own **DARLING CAMUS** !!!
Mitchell.

PRINTED FOR JOHN HEARNE, 81, STRAND.
MDCCCXXIV.

PREFACE.

Hoc juvat et melli est—is *Frolic and Fun* all the world over, though none of the Literati, who have rendered Horace into English, ever condescended so to translate it.

Frolic and Fun then, with not a small sprinkling of *illuminata,* compose the ingredients whereof we have dished up the GRADUS AD CANTABRIGIAM; or, NEW UNIVERSITY GUIDE: And what Cantab will not *Cantab*-it at the bare reading of the Title-page, and apostrophize us in the language addressed to Horace by his patron, Mæcenas——

" Ni te visceribus meis, Horati,
" Plus jam diligo, tu tuum sodalem
" Hinno me videas strigosiorem."

Thus having anticipated the approbation of all the legitimate sons of our beloved ALMA MATER, whether Freshman, Soph, Bachelor, or Big-Wig; our next care is the choice of a patron, and one too of—' glorious notoriety!' There is such a man, but he dwells not with ἄνδρες ἄτιμοι—*Ignobiles*—*Snobs!*

—No, no, no—he is a lad of more νους and keeps better company; he is to be found amidst the θεοι, and his name is no *Riddle* to us—we, therefore, commit our book to his auspices—*Diis charus ipsis*—' Let him look to it !'

We will make bold to assure him, that it will be found more perfect, and therefore we presume, more useful, than any work of the kind that has ever made its appearance in the literary horizon; and we entreat him to recommend it to the attention of all the " *Gentlemen of the First Year,*" as a certain Professor designated the *Freshmen,* and they may become as *cognoscent*, in a short period, as men of a higher *standing* have done in years. To those who may peruse the following pages, we would add,

" Read, mark, learn, and inwardly digest them."

But as for CRITICS, or those who dabble in *Criticism*, a profession which DRYDEN, in his *Life of Lucian,* declared ' was become mere *hangman's* work,'—to these we exclaim, in the words of Aristophanes,

βάλλ' ἐς κόρακας. τίς ἔσϑ' ὁ κόψας τὴν ϑύραν ;

DEDICATION.

To all to whom The GRADUS may come, GREET-ING: in an especial manner, to all FRESHMEN of the most ancient and renowned University of Cambridge.

We fain *would* say, *Quod petis, hic est*—* A work of this kind having long been, confessedly, a *desideratum* in English literature. Words will be found in the *Gradus ad Cantabrigiam;* or, New University Guide; which are scarcely known to the many,—this will be no matter of regret to the Freshman, as it will give him a more improved νους. May it please you, my young masters, to become the patrons of this Work? And in the next edition—should such an occasion offer—it shall be our business, as it will be our duty, to

---

* We remember seeing these words, in large gold letters, over a very commodious booth at *Pot*-fair, otherwise called, *Midsummer*-fair; and won-dered, how *a cup of tea and coffee*—for nothing more was promised—could *answer* to *Quod petis!* This, thought we, might suit the sober '*Maudlins*.'† But, on entering, we found, that the words would admit of very *free* con-struction. The *hic* was behind the bar, where sat the *Quod petis*, who *took in the news!*

† Men of Magdalene College, remarkable for their *wine-less* lives. They drink *tea* to excess. This distinguished honour is now claimed by the Queens-men, with whom it is not unusual to issue an At home' Tea and Ves-pers, alias *bitch and hymns.*

render it more worthy of your, and your successors', support. Regard the present, as a well-meant endeavour.

—— Liberius si
Dixero quid, si forte *jocosius :* hoc mihi juris
Cum venia dabis.

In writing to *Cambridge* men, there can be no need of apology for being too much addicted to *joking*. You will perceive, that we have spared no *puns* to gratify you. This species of wit has been, from time immemorial, in request at our most famous University. In the choice of the terms, ycleped *cant*, or colloquial—and in the definitions annexed to them, you will find, that

"Some be of *laughing*, as ha, ha, he."

SHAKSPEARE citing LILLY.

(See *Much ado about Nothing.)*

Some of the conceits, however, it is to be feared, will be found of a contrary nature, viz. very, very *lamentable*. In this department, we have desiderated, in vain, the talents of a passing ingenious JESUIT,* who is omnipotent in *punning*.

* See JESUIT *sub voce*. The *wight* alluded to, is the author of a Defence of the University in its proceedings against W. Frend, M. A. Fellow of *Jesus ;* of which College, the Author likewise, is, if we may judge from his *incomparable* Work, a very *surprising* ' Fellow.' As a specimen of his *puns*, take the following, which ought to have been inserted under the article KIPLING-ISM.——

' A *Kipling* need not fear, where a *Scaliger* might smile in triumph; for what though the eye-balls of a raving pedagogue might wildly stare at the

DEDICATION.

Omne tulit *PUN*-TOM—

We have been indebted, for some very ingenious illustrations, to the *Cambridge Tart*, the *Gentleman's Magazine*,* the *Oxford and Cambridge Monthly Miscellany*, and the *Spirit of the Public Journals*, which have enriched The *Gradus* with some most exquisite pieces of humorous poetry.— We beg to make our bow, with a maxim from our beloved Horace, which we recommend to the especial adoption of all Young Gentlemen about to enter—*in statum pupillarem :*—

> Rectius vives, Licini, neque altum
> Semper urgendo ; neque, dum procellas
> Cautus horrescis, nimium premendo
>   Littus iniquum.

sight of Bus, poor harmless sound! owing to the quick association in the fuming brain, 'twixt *bus* and *blunderbuss*, or any other instrument of *castigation*, (*!!!*) yet be calm, good gentlemen, an error of the printer, you must surely own it, redeemed in the preceding page by the author himself, but be not mortified—See there it—*is*, and cease to vent your idle rage.' In a note, we are told,—' The clamour against the prolegomena of Dr. Kipling, to his fac simile of Beza, has arisen from the insertion of *Pagini*-BUS, for *Pagin*-IS, which appearing in the preceding page, represents the affair in its proper light.'

* Mr. Urban must, however, excuse us, if we express our indignation at the correspondent who has put into the mouth of the Cantabrigians such language as the following.—' Luckily I *cramm'd* him so well, that *honest* JOL-LUX *tipt* me the *coal.*' By ' honest *Jollux*' is meant the Tutor! ' I am sorry, says a correspondent, in reply, ' that a learned University *is* disgraced by such low, nonsensical conversation, which seems better calculated for the purlieus of Chick-lane, or Broad St. Giles's. It was, no doubt, at one of the above places, that Mr. Urban's correspondent, ' honest *Jollux*,' derived the contents of his communication.

GRADUS

AD

CANTABRIGIAM:

OR,

THE NEW UNIVERSITY GUIDE.

A. B. *Artium Bacculator*, sive Baccalaureus. BA-
CHELOR OF ARTS. Various, and—not worth mentioning, have been the etymologies ascribed to the term
BACHELOR. The true one, and the most *flattering!*
seems to be *Bacca Laurûs*. Those who either are, or
expect to be, honoured with the title of *Bachelor of
Arts*, will hear with exultation, that they are then 'considered as the budding flowers of the University ; as
the small *pillula*, or *bacca*, of the *laurel* indicates the
flowering of that tree, which is so generally used in the
crowns of those, who have deserved well, both of the
military states, and of the republic of learning.'—*Carter's History of Cambridge*, 1753.

It is curious, that LAUREAT was anciently an *aca-
demical* title. 'The beastly Skelton,' so called by
Pope*—by the great Erasmus, in a letter to King
Henry the Eighth, pronounced *Britannicarum litera-
rum, lumen et decus!*—was *laureated* at both of our
Universities. The following is an extract from the
Cambridge Register, Anno 1504. ' Conceditur Jo-

* Imitations of Horace.

B

HANNI SKELTONI, *poetæ laureato,* quod possit con-
stare eodem *gradu* hic, quo stetit Oxonii, et quod
possit uti *habitu* sibi concesso a principe.' It has
not been precisely ascertained by the learned Society
of Antiquaries, who have obliged the world with so
many USEFUL discoveries, in what the *dress* of the
LAUREAT consisted beside his crown. A Bachelor
of Arts must reside the greater part of twelve several
terms, the first and last excepted.

The following ingenious and lively paraphrase on
Horace's *Exegi Monumentum,* by that celebrated
Cantab, Kit Smart, will shew that the title of A. B.
is considered as no mean acquisition.

' 'Tis done:—I tow'r to that degree,
    And catch such heav'nly fire,
That Horace ne'er could rant like me,
    Nor is King's Chapel * higher.

My name, in sure recording page,
    Shall time itself o'erpow'r;
If no rude mice, with envious rage,
    The *butt'ry books* devour.

A title too, with added grace,
    My name shall now attend;
Till to the church, with silent pace,
    A nymph and priest ascend.

Ev'n in *the schools* I now rejoice,
    Where late I look'd with fear;
Nor heed the *Moderator's* voice
    Loud thund'ring in my ear.

---

* *Regali* situ pyramidum altius.

Then with Æolian flute I blow,
A soft Italian lay ;*
Or where Cam's scanty waters flow,
Releas'd from lectures stray.

Meanwhile, friend Banks,† my merits claim
Their just reward from you ;
For Horace bids us challenge fame
When once that fame's our due.

Invest me with a graduate's gown,
'Midst shouts of all beholders ;
My head, with ample square cap, crown,‡
And deck, with hood, my shoulders.'

ABSIT. Leave of absence from Hall. See Note on COMMONS.

ABSOLUTION. It is expressly ordered by the statutes, that the Vice-Chancellor shall pronounce *Absolution* at the end of every term.—OBSOLETE! Such is the good order and regularity, may we not *suppose!* that prevails in the University, that there is no occasion to enforce this, with a variety of other statutes respecting discipline?—*Requiescant in pace!*

ACT. "*To keep an* ACT ;" to perform an exercise in the public schools preparatory to the proceeding in degrees. The *act* opens with a *declamation*, which is no sooner ended, than the *opponent* brings forward

---

* ———— Æolium carmen ad *Italos*
Deduxisse modos.
† A celebrated tailor.
‡ ———— mihi Delphica
Lauro cinge volens—comam.

his *arguments,* and the *keeper* of the *act,* or *respondent,* endeavours to *take them off.*

ACT, for ACTOR, the performer of the above part —a candidate for a degree.

ACT's BREAKFAST; a treat given by the act to the opponents* preparatory to their going to *logger-heads.* It is pleasant to see what a good understanding prevails between these *wordy champions.* They do but quarrel in jest, like the gentlemen of the long robe. If it be not prophaneness to paraphrase on Milton, we might say that, at the *act's breakfast,*

They eat, they drink, and in communion sweet,
Quaff *coffee* and *bohea†*—secure of surfeit!

ÆGROTAT. Permission to be absent from chapel and lecture, on account of corporeal indisposition— though, commonly, the real complaint is much more serious; viz. *indisposition of the mind! ægrotat animo magis quam corpore.*

A READING ÆGROTAT. This is an illness which entirely affects the *head;* and "wherein the patient must administer to himself,"—to

Pluck from the memory a rooted *error;*
Raze out the written *blunders* of the brain—

Sunt—*libri,* quibus hunc lenire dolorem
Possis, et magnam *morbi* deponere partem.

* This compliment is now returned by each of the opponents, but consists of 'Tea and turnout.'

† A learned French Physician, who wrote a Latin Poem on *Tea,* ("Thea Sinensis,") says of it,

———— nostris gratissima Musis.

Mathematical, or, as they are called, "Reading Men," (see READING MEN,) commonly sue for *Ægrotats* in December, it being the month anterior to that in which they take their degree, when it becomes, in the very apposite words of Juvenal, (Sat. VII. 96.)

——— utile multis,
Pallere, et *Vinum toto nescire* DECEMBRI.

There is another kind of abstinence which is prescribed by Horace, and which, according to Dr. Wharton, is ' of the greatest consequence, in order to preserve each faculty of the mind in due vigour.'

Qui studet optatam cursu contingere metam—
(Anglice—to be SENIOR WRANGLER.)

Abstinuit Venere—
Let him avoid CASTLE-END.

ALE. Cambridge has been long celebrated for its Ale ; we have ourselves quaffed no small quantities of this inspiring beverage, and remember the rapturous exclamation of a celebrated classic on receiving some dozens of *Audit* stout:

' *All hail* to the *Ale,* it sheds a *halo* round my *head.'*

Among the many *spirited* effusions *poured* forth in its praise by freshman, Soph, Bachelor, and Bigwig, none appears more worthy of record than the following Sapphic ode, from that cradle of the Facete, St. John's College.

In Cerealem Haustum; ad Promum Johannensem.
A. D. 1786.

Fer mihi, Prome, oh! cohibere tristes
Quod potest curas!—Cerealis haustus
Sit mihi præsens relevare diro
                     Pectora luctu.

Hanc sitim sævam celera domare,
Hoc (puellâ absente) leva dolens cor—
Heus mihi curæ, Cereale Donum,
                     Fer medicamen!

Euge! non audis? sibilat fremitque*
Aureum Nectar, fluviique ritu
Aspice a summo ruit ore zethus
                     Spumeus obbæ!

Cernis! ut vitro nitet invidendo
Lucidus liquor! comes it facetus
Cui jocus, quo cum Venus, et Cupido
                     Spicula tingunt.

Nunc memor charæ cyathum replebo
Virginis!—(curæ medicina suavis!)
Hinc mihi somni—ah quoque suaviora
                     Somnia somno!

O dapes quæ lætitiamque præbes
Omnibus vero veneranda Diva!
Tu mihi das, alma Ceres, amanti
                     Dulce levamen!

Hos bibens succos generosiores
Italis testis nihil invidebo,
Hos bibens succos neque Gallicanæ
                     Laudibus uvæ!

* Bottled Ale well up!!

Cum Johannensi latitans suili,
Grunnio, et scribo sitiente labro—
Hos bibam succos, et amica Musis
              Pocula ducam.

ALMA MATER. The Deity presiding over those,
whose happy destiny leads them to the shades of
Granta, to tread the mathematic path of Truth, ἡ
ὁδος της αληθειας, or to wander in the more elegant
parterres of ancient Classic Lore.

    HINC LUCEM ET POCULA SACRA.

" She holds the candle and the sacred cup,
  And as one wasteth, cries, *'Drink t'other up.'*"

A. M. (Artium Magister.) A Master of Arts must be
a B. A. of three years standing, which time is reckoned from the second Tripos Day following his admission ad Respondendum Questioni. There are however certain exceptions (vide Hat, fellow commoner.)
The following spirited imitation of Horace, (book i.
ode 23.) will shew that this degree is held in no
small esteem amongst the sons of Alma Mater.

Happy M. A. sublime degree!
The threat'ning dons unmoved I hear;
For what's a master's voice to me?
No more the dreaded sound I fear.

Unheeded now the lecturer's call,
The chapel bell (once hated sound),
Now *Mole, in vain, in vain, you bawl,
Midst every din I sleep profound.

    * The late chapel clerk and porter of Christ College.

Or should the huntsman's echoing horn
Incite my spirit to the chase;
The SENIOR's low'ring brow I scorn,
And eagerly the sport embrace.

For instance,—'twas but t'other day,
When, without cap or gown elate,
The hated Proctor crossed my way,*
Nor heeded my defenceless state.

Still trembling Cantab never saw
Than D—f—d a more doughty wight,
Nor can our sister Oxford shew
A fiercer guardian of the night.

Place me midst every toil and care,
A hapless under-graduate, still
To fag at mathematics dire,
Subservient to each fellow's will :†—

Love shall attune my plaintive lyre,
Thy praises, Sylvia! still to tell;
Thy voice shall echo in my ear,—
Thy smiles shall in my memory dwell.

ANGELIC DOCTOR. See DR. KIPLING!

ANNIVERSARY DAYS, now called COMME-
MORATION DAYS. On these *Anniversaries,* it was

---

* The Proctor makes a claim of 6s. 8d. on every under-graduate whom
he finds (*inermem*), or without his academicals.

† Tom Warton humorously tells us—

      ' These fellowships are pretty things,

        We live indeed like petty kings.'

The resemblance is certainly great as to authority.

anciently the custom to perform *mass* in commemoration of deceased benefactors!

APOLLO. *(obsolete.)*
> One whose hair is loose and flowing;
> Unfrizzled, *unanointed*, and untied;
> No powder seen——

His Royal Highness Prince William of Gloucester was an APOLLO during the whole of his residence at the University of Cambridge!!—The strange fluctuation of fashions has often afforded a theme for amusing disquisition. 'I can remember,' says the pious Archbishop Tillotson, in one of his sermons, discoursing on this HEAD, viz. *of hair!* 'since the wearing the hair *below* the ears was looked upon as a *sin of the first magnitude;* and when ministers generally, whatever their text was, did either find, or make, occasion to reprove the great *sin* of long hair; and if they saw any one in the congregation guilty in that kind, they would point him out particularly, and *let fly at him* with great zeal.' (*2d Serm.* on *Prov.* xx. 11. 6. And WE can remember since the wearing the hair *cropt*, i. e. *above* the ears, was looked upon, though not as a "sin," yet, as a very vulgar and RAFFISH sort of a thing; and when the *doers* of newspapers exhausted all their wit in endeavouring to rally the new-raised corps of CROPS, regardless of the Noble Duke who HEADED them; and, when the rude, rank-scented rabble, if they saw any one in the streets, whether Time, or the tonsor, had thinned his flowing hair; they would point him out particularly, and "*let fly at him*," as the Archbishop says, till not a shaft of ridicule remained! The tax

upon hair-powder has now, however, produced all
over the country very plentiful CROPS. Among the
Curiosa Cantabrigiensia, it may be recorded, that our
"most RELIGIOUS and gracious King," as he was
called in the liturgy, Charles the Second, who, as his
worthy friend, the Earl of Rochester, remarked,

> never said a foolish thing,
> Nor ever DID a wise one,—

sent a letter to the University of Cambridge, forbid-
ding the members to wear *periwigs*, smoke tobacco,
and read their sermons!! It is needless to remark,
that TOBACCO has not yet made its EXIT IN FUMO,
and that *periwigs* still continue to adorn "the HEADS
OF HOUSES!"————Till the present, all prevailing,
all *accommodating*, fashion of CROPS became general
at the University, no young man presumed to dine
in hall till he had previously received a handsome
trimming from the hair-dresser. The following inimitable imitation of "The Bard" of Gray is ascribed to
the pen of the Hon. Thomas Erskine, when a student
at Cambridge. Mr. E. having been disappointed of
the attendance of his college barber, was compelled to
forego his *commons* in hall! An odd thought came
into his head. In revenge, he determined to give his
hair-dresser a good DRESSING: so sat down, and
began as follows:

> ' Ruin seize thee, scoundrel COE,
>   Confusion on thy frizzing wait;
> Hadst thou the only comb below,
>   Thou never more shouldst touch my pate.
>
> Club, nor queue, nor twisted tail,
> Nor e'en thy chatt'ring, barber, shall avail

To save thy horse-whipp'd back from daily fears
From Cantab's curse, from Cantab's tears.

Such were the sounds that o'er the powder'd pride
Of Coe, the barber, scatter'd wild dismay,
As down the steep of Jackson's slippery lane,
He wound, with puffy march, his toilsome, tardy
way.

In a room where Cambridge town
Frowns o'er the kennel's stinking flood,
Rob'd in a flannel pow'dring gown,
With haggard eyes, poor Erskine stood;

(Long his beard and blowzy hair,
Stream'd like an old wig to the troubled air;)
And, with clung guts, and face than razor thinner,
Swore the loud sorrows of his dinner.
"Hark! how each striking clock, and tolling bell,
With awful sounds, the hour of eating tell!
O'er *thee*, Oh, Coe! their dreaded notes they wave;
Soon shall such sounds proclaim thy yawning grave:
Vocal in vain, through all the ling'ring day,
The grace already said, the plates all swept away."

The Editors of the *Gradus ad Cantabrigiam*, regret that they have not room for the insertion of the
remainder of the ode.

APOSTLES; the xii last on the list of Bachelors
of Arts: a degree lower than the οἱ πολλοι. 'Scape
goats of literature, who have, at length, scrambled
through the pales, and discipline, of the Senate
House, without being *plucked*, and miraculously obtained the title of A. B.' Vide Cambridge Tart,
page 284.

ARGUMENTS. Syllogisms, for the use of the schools. These may be bought *ready made, good as new,* and very REASONABLE! of Maps,* in Trumpington-Street. They are called "Strings" at Oxford.

ASSES' BRIDGE. *Pons Asinorum.* The 5th Prop. 1st Book of Euclid. '*The* ASSES' BRIDGE *in Euclid* is not more difficult to be got over, nor the logarithms of Napier so hard to be unravelled, as many of Hoyle's Cases and Propositions.' (Connoiseur, No. LX.)—*Note.* By " an ASS" is always understood at Cambridge, a *dull animal,* who has no taste for that *enlivening* study the mathematics! Hence many a man of profound classical erudition is set down an ASS!! On the other hand, by the rule of As *in presenti,* it not unfrequently happens, as an egregious " ASS" very sagaciously observes, ' that a *Wrangler* is not one of the two *Senior Optimes* victorious in a conflict, in which the arms are not furnished from the arsenals of Euclid, or Newton.'

——whoso couth, in other thinges, them grope,
Then had they spent al their philosophie.
Chaucer.

Out of *Euclid* they are out of their *element!*—But levity apart. The following observation of an anonymous writer will be found, I am afraid, to be not more severe than just.

' The study of *classical* learning is entirely, or, if not altogether laid aside in most colleges,' (in Cambridge,) ' learned in so *slovenly,* and taught in

* MAPS, *vulgo,* "JOHN NICHOLSON, BOOKSELLER," whose portrait hangs in the entrance to the public Library, in the hey-day of his prosperity was a character of no small importance in Cambridge. ' *Requiescant manes.*

so unscholar-like a manner, as to disgrace both tutor and pupil.* But this is not all. With this study, namely, that of the classics, the study of *divinity*, the end to which every study should be subservient, is rendered to any good purpose, at least, impracticable. In divinity, the present age holds no rank at all: a circumstance which we owe to the exclusion of *classical* learning in our University, which is supplanted by a study, as *useless* for clergymen and lawyers, as it would be useful to a carpenter, or a joiner.'—(*Enormous Expence in Education at Cambridge*, 1788.)—It is easy to discover this writer to have been an "ass" by his *kicking! alias* braying!

ASSESSOR. The Assessor is an officer specially appointed by grace of the Senate, to assist the Vice-Chancellor in his court, in causis forensibus et domesticis.

AUDIT. A meeting of the master and fellows to examine or *audit* the college accounts. A feast in hall succeeds, on which special occasion, is broached that " *aureum* nectar" celebrated under the article Ale. *(quod vide.)* See also Bursar.

BANDS. Linen ornaments, worn by professors and clergymen when officiating; also by judges, barristers, &c. in court. They form a distinguishing mark in the costume of the Proctors of the Universi-

* To our knowledge the Classical Lectureship in most of the Colleges would not be reckoned amongst the *sinecures* even by Joseph Hume, Esq. M. P.: and we are proud to assert, that for profound Critical and Classical Scholars, and deep read and eminent Divines, Cambridge stands all unrivalled!

ties; and the questionists, on admission to their degrees, are by the statutes obliged to appear in them.

BARNWELL AGUE. The French ***.—(*Ray's Collection of Proverbs.*)—The " ague," so called ironically, now rages also at *Castle-End*. *Barnwell*, a small village near Cambridge, seems to have been a notorious place of amorous resort in olden time. In the seeond part of the comedy called, *If you know not me you know Nobody*, or *The Troubles of Queene Elizabeth*—4to. 1632—Hobson, the famous carrier, who is one of the *dramatis personæ*, says,

' Bones-a-me, knave, thou't welcome. What's the newes

At *bawdy* BARNEWELL, and at Sturbridge-fayre ?'

By a decree of Mr. Vice-Chancellor and the Heads of Colleges, An. 1675, it was ordered, that ' hereafter no scholar whatsoever (except officers of the University performing their duty in searching houses), upon any pretence whatsoever, shall go into any house of bad report in BARNEWELL, on pain, for his misbehaviour and contumacy, of being expelled the University.' *Obsolete.*

B. D. (Baccalaureus Divinitatis.) A Bachelor in Divinity must be a M.A. of seven years standing : his exercise is one act (after the 4th year), two opponencies, a clerum, and an English sermon. (See also ten year men.)

BEDMAKER requires no explanation. This office is not confined to *sex*. In justice to the *women*, they have not only been reckoned adepts at making a bed, *secundum* ARTEM, as the phrase is—but, when they have had a mind to it, have shewn themselves very alert in helping to UN-*make* the bed they have made, *secundum* NATURAM! Indeed, these their *natural* parts and endowments were at one time so notorious, or generally known, that, by a most merciless and *unmanly* decree of the Senate, the whole sex was *rusticated!*

' It is enacted, that no woman, of whatever age or condition, be permitted in any college TO MAKE ANY ONE'S BED; or, to go to the hall, kitchen, or buttery, to carry the provision to any one's chamber, unless she be sent for as a nurse; which nurse must be of mature age, good fame, and either wife or widow; but upon no account YOUNG MAIDS be permitted to attend the students' chambers.' This statute was made in 1625. O tempora! O MULIERES! There is no *scruple* in the present *Saturnian* age, respecting the admission of "*young maids*" into " the students' chambers."

BENE DISCESSIT. This phrase is used to signify that the student leaves his college to enter another by the express consent and *approbation* of the master, and fellows. ' It was formerly,' says the late Dr. Farmer, ' by no means uncommon, for a man, after the severest censures of his own college (were he not actually expelled the University) to gain admission into another, from interest, or from party, or sometimes, from the little emoluments which he brought to his new society. This, at length, produced the grace of the Senate in 1732, which put an end to this infamous traffic.'

De migrantibus ab uno collegio in aliud.

By that grace, no one could be entered of another college *ab alio collegio in aliud nisi prius impetratis literis sub chirographo magistri collegii, &c. testantibus de honestâ suâ, et laudabili conversatione.* (See *Europ. Mag. June* 1794. ' *On the Expulsion of John Dennis.*')

BIBLE CLERK, a very ancient scholarship, so called because the student who was promoted to that office was enjoined to read *the Bible* at meal times. Mr. Masters, the learned historian of Corpus Christi College, informs us, that one Kynne, who was president of that college about the year 1379, purchased a large bible at Northampton, while the parliament was held there, which he presented to the college to be read in the hall at dinner time. But it appears to have been a considerable time after, that the office was restrained to any one person, and a salary annexed to it. In 1473, certain lands and tenements in Cambridge and Barton, to the yearly value of 40 shillings, were given to the society of C. C. C. by Richard Brocher, B. D., for the maintenance of a BIBLE CLERK, who was to be called his scholar.

Volens unum scholarem in grammaticâ eruditum, qui fideliter in artibus studere debet, per magistrum et socios eligi, *qui Bibliam leget coram Mro, et sociis in prandio,* aut alias, et in fine lectionis orabit in latinis verbis, primum nominando Mag. Brocher, inter alios, sic docendo—*Anima M̄RI BROCHER requiescat in pace!*

BISHOP. In Cambridge, this title is not confined to the dignitaries of the church; but *port* wine, made *copiously potable* by being mulled and burnt, with the *addenda* of roasted lemons all bristling like angry hedge-hogs (studded with cloves), is dignified with the appellation of *Bishop*.

Beneath some old oak, come and rest thee, my
  hearty;
Our foreheads with roses, oh! let us entwine!
And, inviting young Bacchus to be of the party,
  We'll drown all our troubles in oceans of wine!

And, perfumed with *Macassar* or *Otto* of Roses,*
  We'll pass round the BISHOP,† the spice-
  breathing cup,
And take of that medicine such wit-breeding doses,
  We'll knock *down* the God, or he shall knock
  us *up.*

We'll have none of the stuff that is sung of by
  Accum,
  Half water,—half spirit——
                        Will Sentinel's Poems.

BITCH. *To* Bitch—*A* Bitching Party. (De Tea narratur.) On board of ship these phrases are very common. One would not suppose that they would be current among the members of a learned

---

* " Dum licet *Assyriáque* nardo
    Potamus *uncti?*"

Lord *Peter* says the ancients had nothing like *Otto of roses,* to stenchify a snouter, or neck-rag; and, "touching" the *Macassar,* had that been known, Cæsar had never needed a red night-cap, or a wreath of laurels, to hide his baldness!--Vide *Suetonius.*

  † Better than *Falernian* or *Massic,* only known in perfection in *cloisters* and *Combination-rooms.*

University, except when the parties were HALF SEAS OVER. But the phrase is very common at Cambridge. A young man who performs with great dexterity the *honours* of the tea-table, is, if COMPLIMENTED at all! said to be " an excellent BITCH !" *Proh pudor!*

BLACK BOOK, a gloomy volume, containing a register of high crimes and misdemeanors. In Miller's Humours of Oxford, a Comedy, one of the characters says,

'Sirrah, I'll have you put in the BLACK BOOK, *rusticated, expelled.* I'll have you *coram nobis* at *Golgotha.*' (A. 11. Sc. 1.)

At the University of Göttingen the expulsion of students is recorded on a *black board.*

BOARDS, long wooden tablets on which the names of the members of each college are inscribed according to seniority, generally hung up in the buttery.

BOGS, 'that place where men of studious minds are apt to sit longer than ordinary.' *(Pope's Letters.)* —The *house* appointed for all living. The small and the great go there.

—— omnes eodem cogimur,
Omnium versatur URNA.
HORACE.

To the same purpose Ovid, if the reader has not already *smelt* out the allusion, which, with SIR *Reverence* be it spoken, is a pretty *strong* one.

Serius, aut citius, SEDEM properamus ad unam ;

which has been thus *cleanly* rendered ;

> O lamentable chance! to one vile *seat*,
> Sooner or later, we must all retreat.

The public bogs belonging to the several colleges in Cambridge are well worthy the inspection of the curious. Persons of *sense* and *taste* will be charmed with the *sweetest* sonnets, and other extemporaneous *effusions,* which have been *vented* with *ease*—the poet sitting all the while, like an oracle on a tripod, and not able to *contain* himself for INSPIRATION!

BORE, probably from Βαρος *onus, molestia*—whence BURDEN. Whatever is odious and disagreeable, however lawful and right, constitutes a BORE—a great BORE—an uncommon BORE—a horrid BORE —an in intolerable and d——lish BORE. For instance, chapel at six o'clock on a hard frosty morning—*(E lecto exsilientes, ad subitum tintinnabuli pulsum, quasi fulmine territi.)*—Likewise, chapel at six o'clock in the evening, which interferes with other *engagements.* Quis non te potius BACCHE. *Hor.*—Other BORES are to attend a sermon at St. Mary's on a Sunday—to *keep an act*—to *cap* a *fellow*—(This *cede majoribus* is reckoned a "terrible BORE!")—Also, to wear bands—to dine in hall—to pay a bill—to subscribe the xxxix Articles, &c. &c. &c. &c. &c. &c.

To BORE; to tease incessantly—to torment—to weary or *worry.* Thus your 'mere mathematician,' whom Sir Thomas Overbury, in his 'Characters,' de-

c 2

fines, "an intelligible *Asse!*" will BORE you over a bottle with Newton's Principia.

> Indoctum, doctum que, fugat recitator acerbus,
> Quem vero arripuit, tenet, occidit que *legendo*.

But the most BORING of all animals is what is called a TICK, one who will stick closer than a brother.

> Non missura cutem—hirudo.
>
> *Hor*.

It has been proved by quotation from Shakspeare, that the word (BORE), in the above sense, is not peculiar to the moderns. In the historical play of Henry the Eighth, the Duke of Buckingham says to Norfolk, alluding to Cardinal Wolsey,

> I read in his looks
> Matters against me, and his eye revil'd
> Me, as his object: at this instant
> He BORES me with some trick.

Consult *all* the editions! *cum Notis variorum!*

BOSKY, 'vino gravis titubare videtur.' Devotees of Bacchus, or rather of Bishop, or peradventure of audit ale. This term is generally applied to those gay sparks, who, elevated by various compotations, are ripe for a lark; and has had various conjectures relative to its derivation, some arguing that it is of Italian ancestry, quasi, bosco, fine, gay; others asserting it to be of Grecian origin, a βοσκω, pasco—to feed like an ox, *viz.* to make a beast of one's self.

'Now when he comes home *fuddled*, alias *Bosky*. I shall not be so unmannerly as to say his Lordship

ever gets drunk either on his club night or from St.
Stephen's,' &c.—*The Sizar*.

BULL DOGS. Formerly applied to the students of
Trinity. (Vide Clarians.) This distinguished appellation is now the *nom de guerre* of the Proctor's satellites.

BURSAR. *Bowser, Bouser,* or *Bourser,* in a Col-
lege; a Gal. BOURSE *a purse.* (*Minshew.*) So in
Thre Sermons preached at Eton College, by *Roger
Hutchinson,* 1552, printed in 1560. B. L.

' Maisters of Colleges do cal their stewardes, and
BOWSERS, to an accompt and audit, to know what
they have received, and what they have expended.'

BURSARS, in short, are the *æruscatores magnæ ma-
tris.* The sixth statute of Trinity College enjoins, that
they, the Bursars, are to receive the college rents,
and to put them into the treasury;—from thence, to
take out what is for the daily and necessary expense
of the college, and to write down the sum, and the
day of the month, with his own hand, in an accompt
book to be kept for that purpose! ' Nothing like this,'
says Sergeant Miller, in his Account of the University
of Cambridge, (*Lond.* 1717, *p.* 106.) ' is ever practised.' He adds; that ' another part of their duty is
to take care that there be wholesome meat and drink;
which,' he says, ' is wholly neglected by them.'

BUTTER " *a* BUTTER;" a *size* or part of butter.
(See *Size*.) " Send me a roll and two *Butters*."

BUTTERY; the House of COMMONS; or place

where bread, butter, cheese, ale, &c. are sold by
retail.

> Be mine each morn, with eager appetite,
> And hunger undissembled, to repair
> To friendly BUTTERY ; there, on smoking crust,
> And foaming ale, to banquet unrestrain'd,
> Matinal breakfast!
>
> *(Panegyric on Ale.)*

When the 'punishment obscene,' as Cowper, the poet,
very properly terms it, of *flagellation,* was enforced
at our University, it appears that the BUTTERY was
the scene of action. In the Poor Scholar, a Comedy,
written by Robert Nevile, Fellow of King's College in
Cambridge, London, 1662, one of the students having
lost his gown, which is picked up by the president of
the college, the tutor says, ' If we knew the owner,
we'd take him down to th' BUTTERIE, and give him
due correction.' To which the student, *(aside,)*
' Under *correction,* Sir; if you're for the *Butteries*
with me, I'll lie as close as Diogenes in dolio. I'll
creep in at the bung-hole, before I'll *mount a barrel,*'
&c. (*A. II. Sc.* 6.)—Again; ' Had I been once i' th'
Butteries, they'd have their rods about me. But let
us, for joy that I'm escaped, go to the Three Tuns
and drink a pint of wine, and laugh away our cares.

> *(Sings.)* We'll carouse in Bacchus' fountains '
>   hang your beer and muddy ale;
> 'Tis only sack infuses courage when our spirits
>   droop and fail.

'Tis drinking at the *Tuns* that keeps us from ascend-
ing *Buttery* barrels, &c.'

BUTTERY BOOK; a register of names of all the Members of the College.

BUZZ. This term will be best explained and illustrated by the subsequent relation. ' What surprised me most, and, I am free to confess, nettled me a little, was the following incident. A pert jack-a-napes at my elbow, who had just helped himself to half a glass of wine, briskly pushed towards me the decanter, containing a tolerable bumper, and exclaimed " Sir, I'll *buzz* you : come, no heel-taps !" Not understanding the phrase, I required an explanation of this extraordinary conduct; when my friend, the president, replied, that *I must drink up the whole,* for such was the custom.' (See *An Account of a Visit to Cambridge, in the Gent.'s Mag. vol.* 64.)

BYE-TERM. Students who take the degree of A.B. at any other time save January, are said to— ' *go out in a bye-term.*'

CANTAB. The much envied title of every son of Alma Mater—see Student, Undergraduate, &c. We cannot here omit the facetious Oxonian's paraphrase of the following line:

CANTAB-*it* vacuus coram Latrone viator.

The coinless Cantab laughs the pad to scorn.

TO CAP. (1.) To touch the cap *en passant* in token of dutiful submission, whether it be to the Vice-Chancellor as supreme ; or, unto Proctors, as unto them that are sent by him for the punishment of evil doers. (2.) To pull off the cap, and make

obeisance *aperto capite,* in the academic phrase.
(See BORE.)—*Capping* appears to have been carried
to the highest, or rather LOWEST, pitch of perfection, in old Catholic times. Thus in a work entitled,
*Sacrarum Ceremoniarum seu Rituum Ecclesiasticorum
S. ROMÆ ecclesiæ Libri tres .. Romæ MDLX** one
part treats ' of the reverence which a Cardinal is enjoined to pay the Pope.' To transcribe the whole
would require no small portion of that *Cardinal*
virtue, PATIENCE. Take, however, a part, and wonder, and *smile !*

Cum ante illius faciem ex opposito venit, firmans
se et manibus extensis, ab anteriori parte *cappam*
capiens, manus sic cappa involutas elevans simul
jungit ante pectus, et profunde caput et humeros
inclinat. These would be no bad directions for
throwing a somerset !—Among other matters of *equal
importance,* the same work treats of *de modo et forma
claudendi et aperiendi os ! ! !*

CAPUT. The Caput, or University Council, consists of the Vice-Chancellor, a Doctor in each of the
faculties, divinity, law, and physic, and two Masters
of Arts, who are the representatives of the Regent
and Non-regent houses. Every grace and supplicat
must pass this body before it can be proposed in the
Senate.

* ' There are many more editions of it. At Venice, 1506; at Cologne,
1572; and there again 1574, in 8vo. Whoever desires to be informed and
convinced of the many *ridiculous,* as well as impious, Roman superstitions,
and the prodigious Papal pride, should get that book.'—*Bishop Barlowe's
Choice of Books in the study of Divinity.* See also ' Emancipation,' a Poem,
1823.

M.A.   Nobleman.   Proctor and his Man.   D.D.   LL.D.   MD

CASTLE END; a place situated at the extremity of the town, of *equal* fame with *Barnwell*, of olden time. This place receives frequent visits from the *Proctors*.

TO CAT, to vomit from drunkenness. (*Grose's Dictionary of the Vulgar Tongue.*) *Vulgo*, he has shot a Cat, or catted.

CATHARINE PURITANS; Members of Catharine Hall, from Καθαιρω. It is grievous to see how the men of one College delight in putting A-PUN (upon) each other.

CAUTION MONEY; a deposit in the hands of the tutor at entrance by way of security. 'The genteel amercements of a young man of fashion in a silver tankard, or in his CAUTION MONEY, ought not, in any wise, to be considered as part of his education.' (*Remarks on the enormous Expence of Education at Cambridge*, 1788.)

The caution of a nobleman is . . . 50*l.*
     a fellow commoner . 25*l.*
     a pensioner . . . . 15*l.*
     a sizar . . . . . 10*l.*

At all Colleges there are also additional fees; those paid at Clare Hall are, for a fellow-commoner, 17*s.* 6*d.* —pensioner, 11*s.* 6*d.*—sizar, 6*s.* 4*d.*

To CHALLENGE . . . . . ΛΟΓΙΚΩΣ αλλ' ουκ ΟΠΛΙΤΙΚΩΣ. (S. Greg. Nazianz. Orat. de Pace. p. 220. ed. Paris.) To invite to a tilt o' the *wits*—a

beating of the *brains*. In 1532, two " pert Oxonians,"
furnished with

> ' captious art,
> And snip-snap short, and interruption smart,
> And demonstrations thin, and theses thick,
> And major, minor, and conclusions quick—'
>
> *Pope.*

took a journey to Cambridge, and, in the public
schools, CHALLENGED any to dispute with them on
the following questions.

> *An jus civile sit Medicinâ præstantius?*

In English, as much as to say—*Which does most*
EXECUTION, *civil law or medicine?!!*—A nice point.
The other question which formed the subject of
serious argumentation was the following :

> *An mulier condemnata, bis ruptis laqueis, sit tertio*
> *suspendenda?*

This is *civil* law with a *vengeance!*

RIDLEY, afterward bishop of that name, was one
of the opponents on this interesting occasion; who
administered the FLAGELLA LINGUÆ to one of these
pert pretenders to logic lore with such happy dexterity, that the other was afraid to *set his wit upon*
him!

CHANCELLOR, an honorary, rather than an
efficient, office, which endures for two years, but is
generally extended by sufferance to the term of life.

CHAPEL CLERK. In some Colleges it is the
duty of this officer to *mark* the men as they enter

chapel; in others he merely sees that the proper lessons are read, by the students appointed by the Dean for that purpose.

CHRISTIANS; Members of Christ, i. e. of Christ College.

CLARIANS; Members of Clare Hall.

So in Kit Smart's Ballad of the Pretty Bar-keeper of the Mitre, 1741,

Dropt she her fan beneath her hoop,
E'en stake-stuck CLARIANS strove to stoop.

The *men* of Clare Hall are called, likewise, *Greyhounds.* But we are equally at a loss to account for this; as we are for *Johnian Hogs,** and *Trinity Bulldogs;* and wonder what pleasure men can find in *making* BEASTS *of themselves!*

COLLEGE. A society of learned men (a colligo). Colleges, Houses, and Halls, are in Cambridge synonimous, though not so at Oxford. Thus Clare Hall is called, " Collegium, sive domus, sive Aula de Clare."

COMBINATION ROOM; ' a parlour adjoining the hall, where the Fellows daily meet for business, or recreation.' *(Bloomefield's Collectanea Cantabrigiensia.)*—This is not correctly explained. The Fellows do, indeed, daily meet in the Combination Room for " recreation"—*(scil.* to take their bottle, *or two,* of wine after dinner, crack nuts, and *conundrums,*

---

* The curious are referred to the CAMBRIDGE TART, for an ingenious suggestion on the origin of *Johnian Hog!*

&c.*) but not "daily" for "business," which is of a very *serious* nature. See *Convention*.

COMMEMORATION DAY; a day devoted to prayers, and *good living*, i. e. feasting.

'Who leads a good life is sure to live well.'

Old Song.

There is always a sermon on this day. The lesson which is read in the course of the service is taken out of Ecclus. XLIV.—"Let us now praise famous men," &c. The following 'Ode on a College Feast Day,' will hardly be read with dry-*lips*, or *mouths* that do not *water!* Whoever was the author of it, he certainly appears to have been a man of *taste*.

I.

'Hark! heard ye not yon foot-steps dread,
That shook the hall with thund'ring tread?
    With eager haste
    The Fellows pass'd;†
    Each, intent on direful work,   [fork.
High lifts his mighty blade, and points his deadly

II.

But hark! the portal's sound, and pacing forth,
    With steps, alas, too slow,
The College GYPS, of high illustrious worth,
    With all the dishes, inlong order, go:

---

* 'Even doctors, professors, tutors, and lecturers, industriously avoid all topics of discourse connected with the species of learning and science which they profess, and most agreeably condescend to expatiate in the *Common* and *Combination-Room*, on dogs, horses, and all the refined amusements of Granta, and Rhedycina.'—(*Dr. Knox.*)

† Qu. paced.—*Printer's Devil.*

In the midst a form divine,
Appears the fam'd sir-loin;
And soon, with plums and glory crown'd,
Almighty pudding sheds its sweets around.
Heard ye the din of dinner bray?
Knife to fork, and fork to knife;
Unnumber'd heroes, in the glorious strife,
Thro' fish, flesh, pies, and puddings, cut their destin'd
way.

III.

See, beneath the mighty blade,
Gor'd with many a ghastly wound,
Low the fam'd sir-loin is laid,
And sinks in many a gulf profound.
Arise, arise, ye sons of glory,
Pies and puddings stand before ye;
See the ghost of hungry bellies
Points at yonder stand of jellies;
While such dainties are beside ye,
Snatch the goods the gods provide ye;
Mighty rulers of this state,
Snatch before it is too late;
For, swift as thought, the puddings, jellies, pies,
Contract their giant bulks, and shrink to pigmy size.

IV.

From the table now retreating,
All around the fire they meet,
And, with wine, the sons of eating,
Crown at length their mighty treat:
Triumphant Plenty's rosy graces
Sparkle in their jolly faces;

And mirth and cheerfulness are seen
In each countenance serene.
  Fill high the sparkling glass,
    And drink th' accustom'd toast;*
    Drink deep ye mighty host,
  And let the bottle pass.
Begin, begin the jovial strain;
    Fill, fill the mystic bowl,
  And drink, and drink, and drink again;
    For drinking fires the soul.
But soon, too soon, with one accord, they reel;
  Each on his seat begins to nod;
All conquering Bacchus' pow'r they feel,
  And pour libations to the jolly god.
At length with dinner, and with wine, oppress'd,
Down in the chairs they sink, and give themselves
    to rest.'

COMMENCEMENT. That period just previous to the close of the Easter term, at which the higher degrees of D. D., LL. D., and M. A., &c. are generally conferred, which precedes by a few days the long vacation. Now also the University prizemen recite their productions publicly in the Senate-house; and the ancient Alumni of Granta revisit the scenes of their early labours and well-earned honours. Commencement Day is always the first Tuesday in July.

COMMISSARY, is an officer under the Chancellor, who holds a court of record for all privileged persons and scholars under the degree of M. A. In

* Fellows of Colleges are not so destitute of *feeling* as to forget their OLD FRIEND!"

this court all causes are tried and determined by the civil and statute law, and by the custom of the University.

COMMONS, a College ordinary.—Bishop Atterbury writes to a lady as follows :

' From Newington, Madam, I rode like a Newmarket racer, to pay a visit to my tutor at Oxford, who, after treating me in the most hospitable manner with a college COMMONS, so soon as we had dined, he readily accompanied me to Woodstock.'

The following is a very surprising statement. It is an extract of a letter from Dr. (afterward Archbishop) Whitgift, of pious memory, to Mr. Secretary Cecil, the celebrated Lord Burleigh.

' That preferment that I have, whatsoever it is, I have it by your honour *his* means, and therefore I owe myself wholly unto you. But it is not so much as is reported. *The Mastership of* PEMBROKE HAL *is but* 4*l.* THE YEAR, *and* 18*d.* THE WEEK FOR COMMONS. My benefice is one of the least in al the dioces. My lecture is the whole stay of my lyuing. My debts are more than I shall ever, being in the state I am, be able to discharge, and extreme necessity, not any prodigality, hath brought me into them.' *(Appendix to Strype's Life of Archbishop Whitgift.)*

To be put out of COMMONS : ' One of the most idle and anile punishments,'—' the most futile and low conceited that Popery ever invented : a punishment inflicted, rather on the parent, than the young

man, who, being *prohibited to eat in hall,* is driven
to purchase a dinner at a tavern, or coffee-house.'
—*(Enormous Expence in Education at Cambridge.)**

COMMORANTES IN VILLA. Masters of Arts,
or those of higher degree, who, residing within the
precincts of the University, enjoy the privilege of
being members of the Senate, without keeping their
names on the College boards. The description of
these persons is, Doctor vel magister commorans in
Villâ qui alit familiam;—which gave rise to the following jeu d'esprit: At a keenly contested election
for the University, when votes were very severely
scrutinized by the contending parties, a gentleman
more remarkable for his parsimony than his learning
tendered his vote. One of the opposite party disputed his qualifications, upon which the candidate,
whose interest he espoused, insisted that he was
Doctor commorans in villâ qui alit familiam. 'That
I deny (replied the other), ALE IT! why he does not
even SMALL BEER IT in his family.'

COMPOUNDER. A person whose living, or liv-
ings, ecclesiastical, of what kind soever, are rated

---

* *" To be put out of Commons;"*—a man is *not* necessarily deprived of the
privilege of dining in hall, on the contrary, he may ' eat till he is red in the
face;' but he is not allowed to have any *dainties,* viz. tartlets, etc. from the
kitchen. 'Tis on the following account it operates as a *punishment:*—By the
statute, a man must *keep* the greater part of *each* term, and by the regulations
of his college, he must dine a certain number of days *in hall,* each week, generally five. No day counts during the time he is " out of commons," nor is
he *marked,* being considered *absent;* so that, if he be *out* three days, he loses
the *week;* and, if he has it *not* to spare, his *term.* But the Tutor can restore
him the *time,* by signing for him what is termed an ABSIT.

to the yearly value of 40 marks in the book of first-fruits or subsidy, and whose living temporal has been demised *communibus annis* at that rate or rent, or by common estimation accounted yearly worth the sum of 40 marks.

COMPOUNDER GRAND. See Grand Compounder.

CONCIO AD CLERUM. An exercise or Latin sermon, which is required of every candidate for the degree of D. D. In cases of non-performance, the sum of 10*l.* is forfeited to the University chest.

CONGREGATION. An Assembly held in the Senate House, for the conferring degrees, and the dispatch of University business in general. There are eleven congregations appointed to be held annually by the statutes; one upon the last day of each term, two on the 10th of October, one on the 3d, and one on the 4th of November, two on the day after the second Tripos, and two on the 11th of June.*

CONSISTORY COURT, of the Chancellor and of the Commissary. For the former the Chancellor, and in his absence the Vice-Chancellor, assisted by some of the heads of houses, and one or more doctors of the civil law, administers justice desired by any member of the University, &c. In the latter, the Commissary acts by authority given him under the

* Any number of members, not less than twenty-five, with the proper officers or legal deputies, at all times however constitute a congregation, and may proceed to business.

seal of the Chancellor, as well in the University, as at Stourbridge and Midsummer fairs, and takes cognizance of all offences, &c. The proceedings are the same in both courts. *(Vide Cambridge Calendar.)* There is an appeal from the judgment of these courts to the delegates of the Senate.

CONVENTION. A court *clerical,* consisting of the Master and Fellows, who sit in the *Combination Room,* and pass sentence on any young offender against the laws of soberness and chastity. By the civil laws of the land, drunkenness is admitted as an extenuation of any irregularity. *Ebriis quandoque venia dari solet derelinquentibus,* tanquam sepultis, et nescientibus. To the same effect, we are told by Calvin; *Jure nostro pœna minuitur, quod in ebrio dolus abesse.* But this is not *University* law! a circumstance which is mentioned with the sole view of its operating as a caution to the young student to drink no more than *stands* to *reason—(scil.)* lest he *fall.*

COOL, impudent, unembarrassed. *"A cool hand,"* in the words of Sir Thomas Overbury, ' one who accounts bashfulness the wickedest thing in the world, and therefore studies impudence.' The following ingenious imitation of the 22d Ode (1 B.) of Horace is dated Cambridge, August 1, 1750.

' On the Happiness of a good Assurance.'

' Whoe'er with frontless phiz is blest,
Still, in a blue, or scarlet vest,

May saunter through the town;
Or strut, regardless of the rules,
Ev'n to St. Mary's, or the Schools,
    In hat, or poplin gown.

A *dog* he unconcern'd maintains,
And seeks, with gun, the sportful plains,
    Which ancient Cam divides;
Or to the *Hills** on horseback strays,
(Unask'd his tutor,) or his chaise
    To fam'd Newmarket guides.

For in his sight whose brow severe,
Each morn the coffee-houses fear,
    Each night the taverns dread;
To whom the tatter'd Sophs bend low,
To whom the gilded tassels bow;
    And Graduates nod the head.

Ev'n in the Proctor's awful sight
On regent walk, at twelve at night,
    Unheedingly I came;
And though, with WHISH's claret fir'd,
I brush'd his side; he ne'er enquir'd
    My College, or my name.' &c.

COPE. The Ermined robe worn by a Doctor in the
Senate-House, on Congregation Days, is called *Cope.*

COPUS   Of mighty ale, a large quarte.
                                    Chaucer.

" Vast *toasts* on the delicious lake,
        Like ships at sea, may swim,"
Laden with nutmeg

* See THE HILLS.
D 2

The conjecture is, surely, ridiculous and senseless, that Copus is contracted from *EPISCOPUS*, a bishop 'a mixture of wine, oranges, and sugar.' *Dr. Johnson's Dictionary.* A *Copus* of ale is a common fine at the Student's table in Hall, for speaking Latin, or for some similar *impropriety!*"*

The following spirited effusion would induce us to suppose that Copus has been naturalized at Oxford as well as Cambridge; but on a *reperusal*, we shrewdly suspect that we can recognise the *vis animi et gutturis* of a congenial and bibilous Cantab, with whom we have ourselves discussed—not a few Copuses.

Invitatory.

Hor. lib. 1. *Od.* 20.

Oh, come to my chambers thou prince of all editors,
　Come and quaff a huge Copus of Magdalen stout;
'Twas bottled the day when the world became debitors
　　To you for the Mag† which beats North‡ out and out.

The *Varsities* laud you, by big wig and commoner,
　Your praises are echoed from Isis to Cam,
Then why, dearest Pere, this humbug and gammon, for,
　Your gout and rheumatics we know's all a flam.

* *Tempora mutantur.* By an old statute, the Students of Trinity College are enjoined to speak no other language at meals than *Latin, Greek,* or Hebrew!!

† Brighton Magazine.　　　‡ Blackwood's.

What tho' à la *Kitchener* dishes wont greet you,
  Still of solids and fluids stores mighty we own:
And all hands and hearts are distracted to meet you;
  Then hasten to Magdalen, " 'Ω ἄναξ ἄνδρων!"

COVER-A**E-GOWN, better known as Bum-curtain, one, like the toga of the Romans, without sleeves. An Undergraduate's gown at St. John's, Sidney, Benet, Emmanuel, Christ's Caius or Gonville, Magdalene and Pembroke.

COURTS. The squares or areas into which each College is divided. For an account of the *last* court. (See Bogs.) These divisions in Oxford are called quadrangles. Vulgo. Quads.

TO CRAM.—(' Knowledge is as food.' *Milton.)* —Preparatory to *keeping* in the schools, or standing examination for degrees, those who have the misfortune to have but weak and *empty* heads, are glad to become '*foragers* on others' wisdom :' or, to borrow a phrase from Lord Bolingbroke, to get their ' magazine of memory *stuff'd*' by some one of their own standing, who has made better use of his time.

The following passage from Shakspeare will furnish the most apposite illustration :

You CRAM these *words* into mine *ears,* against
  The *stomach* of my *sense.*

                            Tempest.

One would think that MILTON alluded to a College CRAMMING, when he spoke of ' *knowledge,* for him that will, to take and SWALLOW DOWN at pleasure, *(glib and easy)* which, proving but of bad *nourishment* in the *concoction*, as it was heedless in the DEVOURING, puffs up, unhealthily, a certain big face of *pretended* learning.' *(On Divorce.)*

TO CULMINATE; to mount a coach-box. The University bucks are then in the meridian of their glory.

CURATORS. The persons who have the care of the botanical gardens and Fitz-William museum, are thus designated in our University.

TO CUT; to look an old friend in the face, and affect not to know him; which is the CUT-DIRECT!

To look any where but AT him—which is the CUT-MODEST, or, CUT-INDIRECT!

To 'forget names with a good grace'*—as, instead of Tom, Dick, or Harry, to address an old friend, " Sir," or, " Mister,—*What's your name ?"* This is the CUT-COURTEOUS.

"Good den Sir Richard."—God-a-mercy fellow !"
And if his name be George, I'll call him Peter;
For new made honour doth forget men's names.
Shakspeare's King John.

To be intentionally engaged on the *phenomena* of the heavenly bodies, when an old friend passes, is the CUT-CELESTIAL.

Lastly, to *dart* up an alley, *dash* across a street,

* *Ben Jonson. Epigrams.*

whip into a shop, or do any thing to avoid the *trouble* and mortification of nodding the head to some one, whom, perhaps, you have as *much* reason to dislike, as the man in the epigram—

Non amo te—*nec possum dicere quare*—This is the CUT-CIRCUMBENDIBUS!

The art of *cutting* an acquaintance is of very considerable antiquity. In a comedy which was publicly acted by the students of St. John's College, Cambridge, in 1606, the following dialogue occurs, which is very *smart* and CUTTING!

"THE RETURN FROM PARNASSUS."

[*See Dodsley's Old Plays.*]

Actus 2. *Scena* 5.

Between Academico and Amoretto.

Acad.—God save you, Sir.

Amor. [*Aside.*] By the mass, I fear me I saw this *genus et species* in Cambridge, before now. *I'll take no notice of him.* By the faith of a gentleman, this is pretty elegy. Of what age is the day, fellow?—Sirrah, boy, hath the groom saddled my hunting-hobby? Can Robin Hunter tell where a hare sits?

Acad. See a poor old friend of yours of S———— College, in Cambridge.

Amor. Good faith, SIR, you must pardon me. *I have forgotten you.*

Acad. My name is *Academico,* Sir; one that made

an oration for you once on the Queen s day, and a show that you got some credit by.

Amor. It may be so; it may be so; but *I have forgotten it.* Marry, yet I remember there was such a fellow that I was very beneficial unto in my time. But, however, *Sir*, I have the courtesy of the town for you. I am sorry you did not take me at my father's house; but now I am in exceeding great haste; for I have vowed the death of a hare that was found this morning musing on her meaze.

Acad. Sir, I am emboldened by that great acquaintance that heretofore I had with you, as likewise it hath pleased you heretofore—

Amor. Look, Sirrah, if you see my hobby come hitherwards, as yet, &c. &c.

TO CUT GATES ; to enter college after 10 o'clock —the hour of shutting them—an offence which is compounded for by fine, which goes to the porter.

> —bars and bolts
> Grow rusty by disuse, and massy gates,
> Forgot their office, op'ning with a touch.
>   *Cowper's Task.*

The following query was addressed some years ago to the University: " Whether the statute which enjoins *the gates* to be *shut* at 8 o'clock in the winter, and at 9 in the summer, be duly observed?" which received the following curious answer;—" They are *generally* well observed; *only!* some use more BENIGN INTERPRETATION, and call it 8 till 9 in the winter; and 9 till 10 in the summer!!"

TO CUT CHAPEL; to be absent—Another offence which is compounded for by fine, which goes
to the Dean.

> ———St. Peter, unto whom are given
> The keys for letting people into heav'n,
> Ne'er got more *ha'-pence* in his life.
> *P. Pindar.*

"I could mention a gentleman, formerly Dean of one
of the larger Colleges, who has amassed a considerable sum of money by *fines on young men for non-
attendance* on prayers."*
> *Enormous Expense in Education at Cambridge.*

In old time the absentees were punished by what is
called *stanging*—making them ride on a colt-staff, or
pole. STANG, in the Anglo-Saxon language, signifies
a wooden bar. This mode of punishment is certainly
ridiculous, and only fit for *children.*—See MEN.

TO BE CUT; to be half seas over. *(See Ray's
Proverbs.)*—" He has *cut* his leg"—periphrasis, *He is
drunk.* 'I remarked, says a visitor to Cambridge,
'that they frequently used the word CUT in a sense to
me totally unintelligible. A man had been *cut* in
chapel, *cut* at afternoon lectures, *cut* in his tutor's
rooms, *cut* at a concert, *cut* at a ball, &c. Soon, however, I was told of men, *vice versâ*, who *cut* a figure,
cut chapel, *cut* gates, *cut* lectures, *cut* hall, *cut* examinations, *cut* particular connexions; nay, more, I was
informed of some who *cut* their tutors! I own I was
shocked at the latter account, and began to imagine

---

* The Deans are by no means eager to exact these fines, but punish
severely by *imposition.*

myself in the land of so many monsters. Judge then, how my horror increased, when I heard a lively young man assert, that, in consequence of an intimation from the tutor relative to his irregularities, his father came from the country to *jobe* him—'But, faith,' added he, carelessly, 'I no sooner learned he was at the Black Bull' (an inn in the town so called), 'than I determined to CUT the old codger completely.' But this was not the worst. One most ferocious spirit solemnly declared, that he was resolved to *cut* every man of Magdalene College; concluding, with an oath, that they were a parcel of *rippish quizzes.*"

Gent. Mag. Dec. 1794.

The passive *cut* is not confined to the University. I meet with it in the same *sense,* which is *sense-less,* in letters of a certain illustrious personage, who has been, as is *here apparent,* as drunk as "a *Prince.*"

'St. L—— has a head like a rock.* We did not carry off less than a *dozen bottles* each (!!!) and he was as sober as a methodist parson. As to my part, I own to you I was d * * * * bly CUT, and made a mistake which had like to have proved fatal to me. I rose early in the morning, to get back to W——r in time, and turning to the wrong stair-case, tumbled over the balustrades,' &c. (*Letters from Florizel to Perdita.*)

CYCLE (κυκλος) is chiefly applied to the nomination of Proctors, and refers to that system of rotation by which those offices are elected.

* The impenetrableness of this "*Saint's*" head is celebrated in the Jockey Club. Dedic. p. 11.

DAY-LIGHT, or Sky-light, is the *easy* attained science of *hard* drinking, when the glass is not a bumper.

D. D. A Doctor in Divinity must be a Bachelor in Divinity of five, or a Master of Arts of twelve years standing. The exercises are one act, two opponencies, a clerum, and an English sermon. When, however, a M. A. takes his Doctor's degree in any of the three faculties, he is said to graduate *per saltum,* though properly this phrase belongs only to the degree of D. D.

DEAN—Udorum tetricus censor et asper.

Mart.

The principal business of a *Dean* is to inflict *impositions* for irregularities, &c. Old Holingshed, in his Chronicle, describing Cambridge, speaks of ' certeine censors, or Deanes, appointed to looke to the behaviour, and manner of the Studentes there, whom they punish *very severely,* if they make any default, according to the quantitye and qualitye of their trespasses.' When *flagellation* was enforced at the Universities, the Deans were *the Ministers of Vengeance.* Antony Wood tells us, that ' Henry Stubbe, a Student of Christ Church, Oxford, afterward a partizan of Sir H. Vane, shewing himself too forward, pragmatic, and conceited, was publicly whipp'd by the Censor in the College-hall." *See* Punishment *passim.*

DEGRADE. De gradu cedere—to put off the evil day—to defer the examination for a year or two.

Some that we have known have taken this dis*honour*-able method of arriving at *honour;* but indeed this *degrading* system cannot with propriety be said to confer *honour!*

> Dabitur licentia sumpta pudenter.
> Ἐπὸς ἄρκει τῷ σόφῳ.

DEGREES. See A. B., A. M., &c. &c.

DESCENDAS. A doutful compliment paid to those unfortunate wights who are appointed to deliver declamations in chapel; but who, not being blest with the eloquence of Cicero or Demosthenes, nor enjoying the retentive memory of Hortensius, by dwelling too long on a single period, are cut short in their harangue by a testy *descendas.* Qu. Descend-Ass!

The following philippic from the pen of the late Lord Byron, on the style of delivering declamations, in Cambridge, is well suited to our subject:

> Or, even perhaps, the Declamation prize,
> If to such glorious height he lifts his eyes.
> But lo! no common orator can hope
> The envied silver cup within his scope;
> Not that our heads much eloquence require,
> Th' ATHENIAN's glowing style, or Tully's fire.
> A manner clear and warm, is useless, since
> We do not try by speaking to convince;
> Be other orators of pleasing proud,
> We speak to please ourselves, not move the crowd:
> Our gravity prefers the muttering tone,
> A proper mixture of the squeak and groan;

No borrowed grace of action must be seen,
The slightest motion would displease the DEAN;
Whilst every staring graduate would prate
Against what he could never imitate.
The man who hopes to obtain the promised cup,
Must in one posture stand, and ne'er look up,
Nor stop, but rattle over every word,
No matter what so it can*not* be heard;
Thus let him hurry on nor think to rest,
Who speak the fastest sure to speak the best;
Who utters most within the shortest space
May safely hope to win the wordy race.

(Vide Camb. Tart. page 67.)

TO DISH AN ARGUMENT; to confute it. 'All
which arguments he *took off*, and completely DISH'D
at last.' *(Gent. Mag.* vol. lxiv. p. 118.)

DOMINUS. A title bestowed on Bachelors of
Arts. DOMINUS *Nokes*—DOMINUS *Stiles.* It has
been disputed by the learned, whether from the above
"DOMINUS" the title of "SIR," which was formerly
prefixed to the names of the Clergy, does not take
its origin. In the Plays of Shakspeare, we meet
with the following characters of the order of PRIEST-
hood. *Sir* Hugh Evans, *Sir* Oliver Martext, *Sir*
Michael, *Sir* Christopher Rerswick; and the Clown
in the Twelfth Night personates *Sir* Topas the Curate.
The following seems to prove incontestibly that this
originated from the DOMINUS at the University. *A
parallel between Cardinal Wolsey, Archbishop of
York, and William Laud, Archbishop of Canterbury,*
1641. 'Both took their degrees according to their
time; and through the whole academy (University),

Sir Wolsey was called, the Boy Batchelor; and Sir Laud, the little* Batchelor.'

DORMIAT. To take out a DORMIAT. *Phr.* a License to sleep. The licensed person is excused from attending early prayers in the Chapel, from a plea of being really *indisposed*—i. e. to attend!

ESQUIRE BEDELS. Gentlemen-ushers to the Vice-Chancellor, who walk before him on all public occasions, bearing each (there are three of them) a silver staff, or mace, on his shoulders, and habited in the dress of his degree, which is usually that of A. M. One of the 'Squire Bedels, likewise, walks before the preacher at St. Mary's, and sees him SAFE into the pulpit! The late Bishop of London, Dr. Porteus, was an *Esquire Bedel* at Cambridge.

EXCEEDING DAY. A dinner *extraordinary;* answering to the *cœna adjicialis* of the Romans. Fuller, the ingenious historian, under the words,

Cantabrigia petit æquales, aut æqualia,

says—' This is either in respect of their *Commons*— all of the same mess have equal shares; or in respect of *Extraordinaries*, they are all ισοσυμβολοι—*club alike.*

EXEAT, vulg. voc. Exit. Leave of absence for the vacation, &c.

EXERCISES. The University Statutes require certain exercises, (as acts, opponencies, &c.) to be

---

* He was *short* of stature, when at full age ; and what may seem strange, he was *shorter* when dead !

performed for particular degrees. *(See Degrees in locis.)*

EXHIBITION; the same with *Scholarship;* a salary sometimes as low as 4*l.* a year, and rarely exceeding 40*l.* in the gift of Schools, Colleges, and City Companies. The first endowment for EXHIBI-TIONS, the learned Baker supposes, was in 1255, when William de Kilkenny, Archdeacon of Coventry, gave 200 marks to the Priory of Barnwell, for the endowment of two *Exhibitions* in divinity. *(Baker's M. S. Hist. of St. John's Coll. Camb.)*—' In times past,' says Latimer, in one of his sermons (An. 1548), ' when any rich man died in London, they were wont to helpe the poore schollers of the Universities with EXHIBITION !' This word in the above sense (an *income*, a *salary)* was not confined to the University. It occurs in Shakspeare, and in Ben Jonson, without any allusion to a *College* life. Thus in *Every Man out of his Humour*, Act ii. sc. 5. ' I'll pay you again at my next EXHIBITION. I had but bare x pound of my father, and it would not reach to put me wholly into the fashion.'—To *exhibit* was used in the same sense formerly. Antony Wood, whose language, as Dr. Berkenhout observes, is antiquated (he might have added, and affected), says of Bishop Longland, ' He was a special friend to the University, in main-taining its privileges, and in EXHIBITING to the wants of certain scholars.'

EXPULSION. A penalty incurred by a too fla-grant breach of the University regulations, and the laws of decorum. This punishment, we rejoice to say, to the honour of all parties, has seldom been inflicted.

*TO FAG. *To learn* AND LABOUR, *truly, to get a living,* and do duty.* *(*Hoc solum in votis habens* OPIMUM SACERDOTIUM.)—'It were some extenuation of the curse,' says Sir Thomas Brown, 'if *in sudore vultus tui* were confinable unto corporal exercitations, and there still remained a paradise, or unthorny place, of knowledge.' *(Vulgar Errors.)*— Dee, the famous Mathematician, appears to have *fagg'd* as intensely as any man at Cambridge. For three years, he declares, he only slept four hours a night, and allowed two hours for refreshment. The remaining eighteen hours were spent in study.

FATHER, or Prælector. One of the Fellows of a College, so called ; who, like Micio in Terence, is PATER *in consiliis,* and attends all the examinations for Bachelor's Degree, to see that there is *fair play,* and that justice is done to the *men* of his own College. See SUPPLICAT.

FELLOWS—*(Socii)—Peers* of the University.

They eat, and drink, and sleep, What then?
They eat, and drink, and sleep again.

Without his joke, not one will pass
My huge rotundity of ——

What food for each sarcastic lubber,
This load of adventitious blubber ;

* This term has been derived by the wits of Cambridge from the celebrated Angle, F. A. G. in the *pons Asinorum.*

Nor less conspicuous, let me tell ye,
Will be my far projecting belly;
Which, thanks to good sirloin and port,
Looks like the bastion of a fort.

The Grumbler.

These fellowships are pretty things;
We live, indeed, like petty *kings*.

T. Warton!!

He trudged along, not knowing what he sought,
And whistled as he went for want of thought.

Cymon and Iphigenia.

In Miller's Comedy called 'The Humours of Oxford,'
a party of *jolly* " Fellows" are introduced, singing as
follows:

' What class of life, though ne'er so great,
   With a good fat *Fellowship* can compare?
We still dream on at our own rate,
   Without perplexing care;
Whilst those, of business when oppress'd,
Lie down with thoughts that break their rest,
     And then, then, then,
   Rise to toil, and slave again.
An easier round of life *we* keep;
We eat, we drink, we *smoke*, we sleep,
     And then, then, then,
   Rise and do the same again.

" We *smoke!*"—This is contrary to statute. (*Vide
Decret. Præfect. Acad. Cant.* 1607.) Nevertheless,
at Emmanuel College, the late Dr. Farmer, among
others, distinguished himself for his TASTE for tobacco!

E.

FELLOW COMMONERS. *Students* (A NON *studendo!)* who are, in *appearance*, the most SHIN-ING men in the University—their gowns are richly trimmed with gold, or silver, lace—their caps are covered with velvet, the tassels to which are of gold, or silver.* These gentlemen enjoy the privilege of cracking their bottle, and their *joke*, if they have one, in the public parlour, or *Combination Room*, where they are literally " Hail, FELLOW, well met." It were almost endless to enumerate the privileges which these gentlemen enjoy by virtue of *hereditary talents*, instilled into their *breeches' pockets*. Those privileges, however, have raised the envy of their inferiors in point of fortune, who, in describing them, seem to have racked their invention to find terms sufficiently indignant. *e.g.*

FELLOW COMMONERS have been nick-named " Empty Bottles !" They have been called, likewise, " *Useless* Members !" "The licensed Sons of Igno-rance !" ' The order of *Fellow Commoner,*' says one writer, 'has, by immemorial usage, a kind of pre-scriptive right to idleness ; and fashion has inspired it with an habitual contempt of discipline !' It is even recorded as the saying of Dr. Watson, the present Bishop of Llandaff, that 'a Fellow Com-moner is of no use, but to the Bed-maker, *Tutor,* and Shoe-black !!!!'†

---

* ' These *gold threads* have almost as much influence in the University as a red or blue ribband at court.' (*See the Connoisseur, No.* 97.)

† Be it known to our readers that this stigma, is no longer, if it ever was, applicable to this class of gentlemen ; many of whom have obtained a distin-guished place in the Tripos : and it is by no means unusual to find their names amongst Medalists and Prizemen.

A.A.P. delt.

Married.   St. Johns.   Emmanuel.   Trinity.   Downing.

FELLOW COMMONERS.

O, mighty Jove, what have I liv'd to see!
Bed-makers and *shoe-blacks* class'd with *me!*

' That Dr. Watson was *Tutor* of a College is known
of a surety. Who can doubt, then, but that his
Lordship spoke from experience?' It is, likewise,
well known, that, in the year 1786, a gentleman, who
had been a *pupil* of his Lordship, Mr. Luther, of
Essex, left him by will the USEFUL sum of 20,000*l.*!!!

FRESH; newly come. So Shakspeare;

> methinks I see
> Leontes op'ning his free arms, and weeping
> His welcomes forth: asks thee the son forgiveness,
> As 'twere i' th' father's person; kisses the hands
> Of your FRESH princess.
> *Winter's Tale, A. IV. Sc. 9.*

Likewise, *awkward, quizzical;* like a Freshman.
Thus in the Archæologiæ Atticæ, Edit. Oxon. 1675.
' For their behaviour at table, spitting and coughing,
and speaking loud, *was* counted uncivil in any but
a gentleman; as *we* say in the University, that nothing is FRESH in a Senior,* and to him it was a
glory.' B. VI.

FRESHMAN.
While Sophs and *Freshmen* trembled at his nod.
Byron.

Nunc adbibe puro
Pectore verba, puer; nunc te melioribus offer.

---

* A Soph.

(Quo semel est imbuta recens, servabit odorem Testa diu.)

Horace.

One who has not been a twelvemonth in the lap of his *Alma Mater.* " I am but a FRESH-water soldier under the banners of Phœbus." We FRESH-water academicians." *(See Ant. Wood's Speech before his Fellow Students on his Entrance at Oxford, in his* " Life."

FRESHMAN'S LANDMARK; King's College Chapel. This stupendous edifice may be seen for several miles on the London road; and indeed from most parts of the adjacent country.

GAUDIES.—(a gaudeo.) Certain elegant ' *set-outs,* when men in their own rooms enjoy the ' *otium cum dignitate,*' ' like hearty good fellows,' there being on such occasions, no lack of *solids,* or Hock, Claret, and Champaigne, to elevate *congenials.*

—— " A soothing balmy blessing,
Sole dispeller of our pain,
Gloomy souls from care releasing,
He who drinks not—lives in vain."

GOLGOTHA; the place of Sculls, where the Heads of Houses sit at St. Mary's in awful array.

GRACE. Any proposition presented to the consideration of the Senate; but, previously to its being voted by the two Houses, it must be read and approved by the Council or Caput, each member of which has a *negative* voice

GRADUATE; one who has taken his degree in any of the learned profession. Oh, fortunate nimium. See *A. B.*

GRAND COMPOUNDER'S; Gentlemen who being blessed with a tolerable competency, enjoy the enviable privileges of paying double fees on their admission *ad respondendum questioni.*

GRANTA. Thus was our famous University called originally.

> Quid quod GRANTA novem dicata Musis,
> Tersis prænitet erudita linguis.
>   (Leland vid. Cygnea Cantio, 1545.)

Granta (says the same great antiquary) Britan-nice *Cair-grant*, Saxonice *Grante-cestre*, and vocabulo recentiori *Grantebrycge*, &c.' Lambard contends, that ' Cambridge Town and University is not the same that Beda' (meaning the venerable Bede) ' calleth *Grantacestre*; for that,' says he, ' is yet known by the name of the Grancyter, and is a small village thereby; but Cambridge is the same that Marian, and others, call *Grantbridge*, and we corruptly, CAMBRIDGE.' (This village' is now called *Grantchester*. According to another great antiquary, it was originally called *Caer-gurgant*,—(from King Gurguntius, the supposed founder;) " in tyme, by contraction of the word, it grew to be cauled *Caer-grant*, which the Saxons cauled *Grant-breig*, which, in tyme, grew to Cambridge." (*Lewis's Ancient History of Great Britain*."

The following Account of the several Colleges in

Cambridge, and the Sciences which were anciently taught in them, is taken from the fourth volume of Leland's Itinerary, by Hearne. (Appendix.)

CANTABRIGIÆ.

Regale Collegium, -	Leg. & cæt. Art.
Regia Aula, - - -	Leg. & Art.
Michael Howse, - -	Theol. & Art.
Gunwel Hawle, - -	Theol. & Art.
Clare Hawle, - - -	Theol. & Art.
Trinite Hawle, - -	Leg.
Benet College, - -	Theol. & Art.
Peter Howse, - - -	Theol. & Art.
Collegium Reginæ, -	Theol. & Art.
Bokingham College,-	Monachi.
Quartuor ordines fratrum,	
Collegium Jesu,	
Fishwick Hostel, - -	Art.
Honyngis Yn, - - -	Leg.
Garret Hostel,	
Gregory Hostel, - -	Art.
S. Magaret's Hostel,	
S. Augustine's Hostel,	Art.
S. Thomas Hostel, -	Art.
S. Barnard's Hostel,-	Art.
S. Clement's Hostel,-	Leg.
Burdon Hostel, - - -	Leg.
S. Maris Hostel,	
Trinite Hostel, - -	Leg.
Harliston Place, - -	Art.
S. John's Hostel, - -	Leg.
S. John's Religiosi,	
S. Paul's Yn, - - -	Leg.
Canonici albi.	

The University at present consists of the following Colleges :—

	A. D.
St. Peter's College, founded - -	1257
Clare Hall - - - - - - -	1326
Pembroke - - - - - - - -	1343
Gonville or Caius - - - - -	1348
Trinity Hall - - - - - - -	1350
Corpus Christi or Benét - - -	1351
King's - - - - - - - - -	1441
Queen's - - - - - - - - -	1446-65
Catherine Hall - - - - - -	1475
Jesus - - - - - - - - - -	1496
Christ's - - - - - - - - -	1505
St. John's - - - - - - - -	1511
Magdalen - - - - - - - -	1519
Trinity - - - - - - - - -	1546
Emmanuel - - - - - - - -	1584
Sidney Sussex - - - - - - -	1598
Downing - - - - - - - - -	1800

GROATS. *To save his groats ;* to come off handsomely.

" At the Universities, nine *groats* are deposited in the hands of an academic officer by every person standing for a degree, which, if the depositor obtains with honour, are returned to him." *(Grose's Dict. of the Vulgar Tongue.)*

GYPS.—(Called Scouts at Oxford.)—Mercuries for expedition and *roguery.* These gentlemen are destined to do as many odd jobs as Scrub, in the Stratagem. Their knowledge of *conveyancing,* which is very *extensive,* is seen in trifling article of waiting at table. They have a great many perquisites. It is doubted whether JACK KETCH gets more suits of clothes, by VIRTUE of his office! They obtained the appellation from their rapacious habits, they not being over scrupulous in breaking the 8th commandment. The word Gyp very properly characterizes them, it being derived from the Greek word ΓΥΨ, a Vulture. (*See Cambridge Tart*, 277.)

HABIT. COLLEGE HABIT.—College dress; called of old, LIVERY : the dress of the Master, Fellows, and Scholars, according to their respective degrees. Notwithstanding the punishment denounced against any Student who shall be seen without his gown and cap, and even band, yet our University bucks, who dislike of all things to be accounted creatures of HABIT, are repeatedly seen strutting about the town, in forbidden boots, with hat, and stick, and eke a *dog!* A modern reformer proposes, that for the first offence (appearing without the college habit) the delinquent shall be *rusticated* six months ; for the second, one year ; for the third, that it may be *capital*, and the delinquent expelled the University.*

HACKS. HACK PREACHERS; ' the common Exhibitioners at St. Mary's, employed in the service of defaulters, and absentees. A piteous, unedifying tribe. (*Gilb. Wakefield. See Memoirs of his Life*, 1792.)

On Sunday, arrogant and proud,
    He purrs like any Tom Puss,
And reads the word *of God so loud,*
    He must be *Theo-pompus.*

Camb. Tart, p. 112.

It must be confessed, however, that these HACKS

---

* The offender is now dished by an Argumentum ad Crumenam, and fined 6s. 8d.

are good fast *trotters*—as they commonly go over the course in twenty minutes, and sometimes less. The following memorial may serve to shew, how much the *patience* of an auditory has declined from what it was in former times.

J. Alcock, divina gratia, Episcopus Elliensis, prima die dominica MCCCCLXXXIII, bonum et blandum sermonem prædicavit, in ecclesia B. Mariæ, Cantabrig. qui incepit in hora *prima* post meridiem, et duravit in horam *tertiam et ultra.*

Dr. Barrow was the last of the family of the *Spintexts.*

HALL. (See College.) Also the House of *Commons,* or place where men of every rank and degree discuss the *good things* of the world.

" How jocund are their looks when dinner calls,
" How smoke the cutlets on their crowded plate."

Oh let not temperance, too disdainful, hear
   How long their feasts, how long their dinners last!
Nor let the fair, with a contemptuous sneer,
   On these unmarried men reflections cast.
                See Cambridge Tart, 82.

HARRY SOPHS; or, HENRY SOPHISTERS; in reality Harisophs, a corruption of Erisophs (ἐρίσοφος, valde eruditus), students who have kept all the terms required for a law act, and hence are ranked as Bachelors of Law by courtesy. They wear a plain, black, full sleeved gown. Many conjectures have been offered respecting the origin of this term, but none which are satisfactory. First, That King Henry the Eighth, on visiting Cambridge, staid all the Sophisters a year, who expected a year of grace should have been given them. Secondly, Henry the Eighth being commonly conceived of great strength and stature, these *Sophistæ Henriciani* were elder, and bigger than others. Thirdly, In his reign, learning was at a loss, and the University stood at a gaze what would become of her. Hereupon many Students staid themselves two, three, some four years, as who would see how their degrees before they took them would be rewarded and maintained. *(See Fuller's Worthies, and Ray's Proverbs.)*—A writer in the Gent. Mag. thinks ' *Harry* quasi Aρα *utique nempe*—a *Soph* INDEED !' He had better have said an *arrant* Soph.

HAT FELLOW COMMONER ; the son of a Nobleman, a Baronet, or eldest son of a Baronet, who wears the gown of a *Fellow Commoner* with *a hat,* and is admitted to the degree of A. M. after two years residence.

HEADS OF HOUSES ; the masters of the different colleges are so called,

In fair round belly with good capon lined,
With eyes severe, and Head of formal cut,
As you like it.

I have fed purely upon ale, I have ate ale, drunk ale, and I always sleep upon ale.—*Beaux Stratagem.*

As what a Dutchman plumps into the lakes,
One circle first and then a second makes ;
What dulness dropt among her sons impress'd,
Like motion from one circle to the rest,
So from the midmost the mutation spreads
Round and more round o'er all the sea of Heads.
Pope's Dunciad.

Vain as their houses, heavy as their ale,
Sad as their wit, and tedious as their tale.
Byron.

HEELTAPS.—The custom of the University is
" to fill what you please, but drink what you fill."
Any left in the glass is called heeltaps, which is
a violation of the rules of good living. *(See Buzz.)*

HIGH STEWARD, The, has a special power to
take the trial of scholars impeached of felony within
the limits of the University, and to hold and keep a
leet according to the established charter and custom.
He is allowed a deputy. This office is now merely
honorary.

HILLS. Gogmagog Hills, near Cambridge; a
common morning's ride.
' Where have you been sporting your *bit-o'-blood?*'
' Just *to the Hills* and back.'

These Hills are of not less notoriety at Cambridge,
mid the sons of Granta, than the celebrated statues
of *Gog* and *Magog* in Guildhall. They raise their
lofty heads about four miles east of Cambridge, and
are the highest eminences in the county. How they
obtained their fanciful appellation is uncertain. It
has been conjectured that some of the students, in
olden time, cut the figure of a giant on the turf, and
named it *Gogmagog.*

On the top of these Hills is a triple entrenchment
with two ditches, rudely circular. Some have supposed this a British, others a Roman camp. Probably it was occupied by both parties. Within the entrenchment, which encloses about $13\frac{1}{2}$ acres, are the
house and grounds of Lord Francis Osborne, son of
the late Duke of Leeds.

HONORS. — Certain distinctions conferred on Gentlemen eminent for their Classical and Mathematical acquirements. *(See Tripos, Wrangler, &c.)*

HUDDILNG. . . Asinus meus habet aures,
Et tu habes aures.
Ergo : Tu es asinus meus.

This, which Sir Thomas More mentions, was ' the forme of argving vsed by yonge children in grammer schooles,' in his time, would be thought very good HUDDLING for old boys at the University. ' When the Students,' says Sergeant Miller, ' come to take the degree of B. A. among other things they swear, that they have learned rhetoric in the first year of their coming to the University; in the second and third, logic; and in the fourth year, philosophy; and that they have performed several other exercises, which, through the multitude of scholars, and the want of time appointed for them, if they are performed at all, they are, the greatest part of them, in the manner which they call HUDDLING—which is in a slighter manner than the usual mootings are in the inns of court.'

It would seem, from the following from Dr. Knox, that HUDDLING was known at Oxford. ' Droll questions,' says he, ' are put on any subject; and the puzzled candidate furnishes diversion by his awkward embarrassment. I have known, he adds, the question on this occasion to consist of an enquiry into the pedigree of a race-horse.'—At Cambridge, the diversion of HUDDLING seldom terminates without some *barbarous* and *wretched* PUNNING.

JESUIT; a Member of Jesus College.

IMPOSITION ; ' an addition of exercise given for a punishment. To *impose* that punishment—Multam imponere. *Imposer cette peine.'—(Lovell's Universe in Epitome*, 1679.)—' Every pecuniary mulct whatever on young men *in statu pupillari*, should be abolished. The proper punishment is employing their minds in some useful IMPOSITION.'—*(Enormous Expense in Education at Cambridge.)*—' Literary tasks, or frequent compulsive attendances on tedious and unim‑ proving exercises in a College Hall.' *(T. Warton. See Milton's Minor Poems by T. W. p.* 432.)

INCEPTORS ; Gentlemen, who have proceeded to the degree of M. A. immediately after the second Tripos-Day; but who not enjoying all the priviliges of M. A. till the commencement, are termed Inceptors.

TO JOBE, to reprove, to reprimand.—*See Ray's Proverbs.* " As poor as Job." ' In the University of Cambridge, the young scholars are wont to call chid‑ ing, JOBING.' " Methinks it could not do any great hurt to the Universities, if the old Fellows were to be JOBED for their irregularities, at least once in four or five years, as the young ones are every day, if they offend." *(Terræ Filius, No. I.)*

JOBATION; a sharp reprimand from the Dean for some such offence as not wearing a band (obsolete); I have known that, after a *jobation* for this *great of‑ fence!* the delinquent has been punished with an *im‑ position!* the not *capping* a superior, though a *fellow!* —the wearing a *green* coat—or a *red* waistcoat—the *cutting* hall, chapel, or gates—*cutting* lecture, &c. &c.

"She tells Dr. Johnson, that when once he turns the page, she is sure of a disquisition, or an observation, or " a little scold." But when do we see any scold, little or great, throughout the two volumes? No such thing is to be found in them. And why? Because she has carefully suppressed every JOBA-TION, *as they say at Cambridge.*" *(Barretti's Strictures on Seigniora Piozzi   Europ. Mag. Vol. XIII. p.* 293.*)*

JOHNIAN HOGS; an appellation bestowed on the Members of St. John's College.—Whence it arose has not been rightly, or with any degree of probability, ascertained. A variety of conjectures are offered in the *Gent. Mag. for* 1795, with the following *jeu d'esprit.* A genius espying a Coffee-house waiter carrying a mess to Johnian in another box, asked, if it was a dish of *grains.* The Johnian instantly wrote on the window,—

Says ———— the Johns eat grains; suppose it true,
They pay for what they eat; does he so too?

Another writer, whom I should suspect to be *May-sterre* Ireland, the pseudo-Shakspeare, has, or pretends to have, discovered the following, in a very scarce little book of Epigrams, written by one Master James Johnson, Clerk, printed in 1613.

To the Schollers of Sainct John his College.

Ye Johnishe men, that have no other care,
Save onelie for such foode as ye prepare,

To gorge youre foule polluted trunkes withall;
Meere SWINE'ye bee, and such youre actyons all;
Like themme ye runne, such be youre leaden pace,
Nor soule, nor reasonne shynethe in your face.

Edmond Malone, Esq. of 𝔅𝔩𝔞𝔠𝔨 𝔏𝔢𝔱𝔱𝔢𝔯 sagacity,
would discover, with half an eye, that the above was
not the orthography of 1613. *Sainct—themme—reasonne—shynethe*, &c. For a farther account. (*See
Cambridge Tart, p. 279.*)

TO KEEP;—to live. "Where do you *keep?*"
Where are your rooms?—" In the way to my friend's,
having quite forgotten the direction to his Chambers
in his College, I asked a Bed-maker, who was peram-
bulating one of the courts, where Mr. ——'s Chambers were, as I understood he lived in that court.
The fellow stared me in the face, with an insipid
vacant look, gradually improving into a grin. I re-
peated my demand in a more impatient tone of voice,
and added, ' I came to dine with Mr. ——.' The
man scientifically shrugged up his shoulders, and
walked away, protesting, he could not tell. I luckily
espied my friend at the other end of the quadrangle,*
and went to him. Upon my mentioning the recent
embarrassing circumstance, he said, with a smile, ' I
ought to have asked for his rooms, or enquired where
he KEPT.' The word in this sense is often used by
old writers."—(*Gent. Mag.*)—Dr. Johnson, in his
Dictionary, cites a very apposite passage from
Shakspeare :—" Knock at the study were they say he

---

* " *Court*" at Cambridge, answers to " *Quadrangle*" at Oxford.

keeps." Sir Thomas More, in a letter to Dean Colet, " says, ' Yff the discommodities of the cittie doe, as they may very well, displease you, yet may the countrie about your parish of Stepney afforde you the like delights which that affordes you wherein now you KEEPE." *(More's Life and Death of Sir Thomas More.)*

To KEEP *in the Schools;* to perform an *act* or *opponency.* (To borrow the words of Sir Richard Steele, in the Dedication of one of his Treatises to the Pope;) ' a game at learned *racket.* The question is the *ball* of contention, and he wins, who shews himself able to keep up the *ball* the longest. A syllogism strikes it to the *respondent,* and a negation, or a lucky distinction, returns it back to the *opponent;* and *so* it flies over the heads of those who have time to sit under it, till the judge of the game strikes it down with authority into rest and silence.'

KING'S MEN. Members of the King's College.

> Ev'n gloomiest *Kings-men,* pleas'd awhile,
> Grin horribly a ghastly smile.
> > *C. Smart.*

A KIPLINGISM; a blunder-BUS levelled at poor Priscian's head by the *learned* Dr. Kipling. The opposition wits at Cambridge have composed an epigram of *Kiplingisms.—(Kiplingius* loquiatur.)

PAGINIBUS nostris dicitis mihi menda quod in sunt, At non in recto vos puto ego esse viri.

Nam primum jurat (cætera ut testimonia *omitto*)
    Milnerus,* quod sum doctus ego et sapiens.
Classicus haud es, aiunt. Quod si non sum? in sacro
    sancta
Non *ullo* tergum verto theologia.

We should be doing injustice to the defunct, were
we not to take cognizance of a modern *Kiplingism*,
vel potius *Monkism*, namely, a lapsus of a late Greek
Professor, whom we beg leave to inform that, despite
his anxiety and care to have the 'damning proofs'
destroyed, we have now in our possession a copy of
the first edition of the ALCESTIS et SERVIBIMUS.†

TO KNOW; a word which is very liable to mis-
construction. "Do you *know* such a one?" i e. Are
you upon terms of great intimacy?—and, Do you
wish to *acknowledge* him as your friend? Though a
buck and a *quiz*, or *raff*, were to dine together at the
same table every day—to meet together, continually,
at wine parties—nay, *keep* together in the same stair-
case; yet, if the former were asked,—Whether he
knew either of the latter? he would answer, with all
imaginable coolness and composure, in the *negative!!*
"There is such a man, but I don't KNOW him."

KNOWING men, or knowing hands. (*vide* Non-
reading Men and cool hands.)

LARK. A spree, a row, any thing *out-and-out*,
whether it consists in upsetting a SNOB, or topping a
five barr'd gate, *boning* a *knocker*, or demolishing a

---

* The late Master of Queen's College.

† For an explanation of these *literæ tenebrosæ*, we beg leave to refer our
readers to the INSERVIBUNT of the *aforesaid* edition.

lamp. The ancient and inveterate antipathy which exists between Gown and Town, has been the prolific source of many a lark; as the following imitation of Horace evidences:

" 'Bout the wars of the *Cantabs** and *Snobs*' rival glory;
    Cease, Peregrine South, to bewilder thy brain;
For their freaks, ' *sine limine* shine will in story,
    Though Camus† divide, they will at it again !"

—We cannot better conclude this article than by citing the following animated description, from the pen of a celebrated Jesuit, of—

THE BATTLE OF PEAS HILL.

' Musa, mihi causus memora, quo numine læso
Quidve dolens *Regina*——
                                                    Virg. Æn. i. 7.
'——— quæque ipse miserrima vidi
Et quorum pars magna fui——
                                                    Æn. ii. 5.
Fortunam *Snobili* Cant—abo et nobile bellum.
                                                    Hor. Ars Poet. 137.

The following effusion was penned the day after the memorable 13th of November, 1820, which must be a day of pleasant recollection to all Cantabs, as long as there shall be a Snob or *Radical* amongst them, or a *fist* to *bate* them with. This is the only *Matriculation-day* which is registered in *letters* of blood in the

---

* ' Quid bellicosus Cantab—er et *Scythes*,'--The " *pole-handers*" of the Cam (the " *Cam pest* res Scythes") are quite as barbarous and as savage as ever the ancient *Polanders* used to be, and may appropriately be called, the *modern* Scythes.

† ' *Adria*, divisus objecto. —Talk of the Cam to a Johnian, and he always thinks of a *dry attic* on the Water-Staircase.

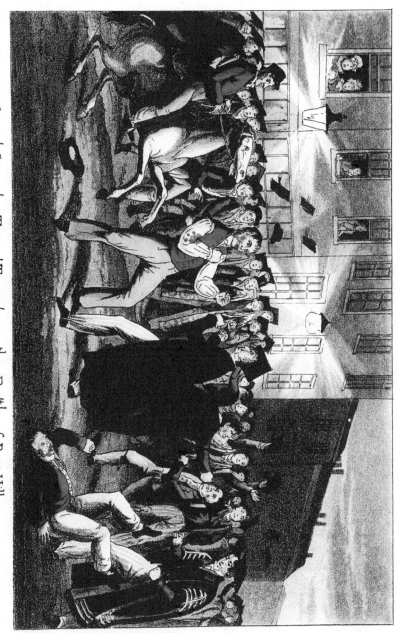

Gown! Gown! —Town! Town! or—the—Battle of Peas Hill.

archives of the Vice-chancellor; and we are sure
there never was, nor ever will be, such an occasion for
calling FRESHMEN from the science of *mechanics* to
the application of its *theory* in the *science of war*.

On GRANTA, when the sun was low,
No symptoms lower'd of fearless row,
But all was silent as the flow
    Of CAMUS rolling *tardily*.

But Granta saw another sight,
When radicals presumed at night,
With *Carter's** mutton-wicks to light
    Their Caroline's base treachery.

Round Hobson's conduit quick array'd,
Each GOWNSMAN rush'd the cause to aid,
And fast about him each one laid,
    With blows that told most terribly.

Then rushing forth the SNOBS among,
Fierce from the ranks the Johnian sprung,
And loud and clear the market rung,
    With shouts of dreadless liberty.

But redder yet shall be each cheek,
And louder yet each tongue shall speak,
And fiercer yet each soon shall wreak
    His vengeance most undauntedly.

'Tis rushlight all—but what can shew
The GOWNSMAN from the GOWNSMAN'S foe,
As shouting in thick files they go
    To battle all so merrily?

* A noted vender of wax, moulds, short sixes, farthing rushlights, and all
other *wick*—ed wares.

No banners there were waving high,
To cheer the brave to victory,
No pennon floating to the sky,
  With rare device wrought curiously.

No plumes of crested pride were seen,
But tassels black of silken sheen,
With gold and silver mix'd between,
  Emblems of unanimity!

No sound was heard of martial drum,
No bugle blast, but one wild hum
Floated o'er all: "the SNOBS! they come,
  On! On! and meet them cheerily."

And then was shout, and noise, and din,
As rallying forwards pourëd in
Hundreds and hundreds, to begin
  The work of fame so gloriously.

Then rush'd undaunted, to the fight,
The tall—the low—the strong—the light;
And, Oh! it was a glorious sight,
  That strife of TOWN and GOWN to see.

As fist to fist, rais'd high in air,
And face to face opposed were,
As shone the conflict in the glare
  Of lights that told of Bergami.

Then rushed to fight the hardy SOPH,
Regardless of the townsmen's scoff,
As one by one they sallied forth
  To war in ambush warily.

Then rush'd the FRESHMAN to essay
His maiden valour in the fray,
And who that valour shall gainsay,
  And wrong not such effrontery ?

Then, with one cry so loud and shrill,
It echoed to the CASTLE HILL,
They charg'd the SNOBS against their will,
  And shouted clear and lustily.

Then all distinctions were forgot—
Then, silk and velvet had one lot
With *tatter'd stuffs*, upon that spot
  Which sacred was to bravery.

No signs of fear, no signs of dread,
Of bloody nose or broken head,
Of wretch by Proctors homeward led,
  For " acting contumaciously."

No thoughts were there, but such as grace
The memory of that crowded place,
The memory of that gallant race
  Who *took* and *gave* so heartily.—

The combat deepens ; on, ye brave,
Who rush to conquest, or to save !
Wave all your *stuffs* and *poplins* wave !
  And charge with all your chivalry !

Few, few, shall part where many meet,
Dull soon shall be each crowded street,
Responsive, now, to thousand feet
  Pursuing on to Victory.

LICET MIGRARI. A permission to leave one's college. This differs from the Bene Discessit, for although you may leave with consent, it by no means follows in this case that you have the approbation of the master and fellows so to do.

LIONS; Strangers, or visitors, at the University.

LITTLE GO. A previous examination in Classics and Divinity, held in the Senate-house, instituted by a Grace of the Senate in 1822, which all Undergraduates are obliged to attend in the Lent Term of their second year.

The following query on the Oxford *Small* Go, lately appeared in *Jackson's Journal*.

Exercise for the Little Go Men.

No Cat has *two* Tails,
A Cat has *one* tail *more* than No Cat,
Ergo. A Cat has *three* tails.

LL. B. A Bachelor of Laws must be of six years standing complete, and must keep the greater part of nine several terms. The exercise is one act.

LL. D. A Doctor of Laws must be of five years standing from the degree of LL. B.; or a M. A. of seven years standing. The exercises are two acts and one opponency.

L. M. A Licentiate in Medicine is required to be M. A. or M. B. of two years standing. No exercise, but examination by the Professor and another Doctor in the faculty.

TO LOUNGE—(Occupatus nihil agendo) to

' waste away,
In gentle inactivity, the day.'

The life of a Lounger is inimitably drawn by Martial in one line.   See ' The Oxford Sausage.'

Prandeo, poto, cano, ludo, lego, * cæno, quiesco.

TO TAKE A LOUNGE; to saunter about the town in listless indolence.

Quacunque libido est
Incedo solus: percontor quanti olus, ac far :
Fallacem Circum, vespertinumque pererro
Sæpe forum, &c.
Perditur hæc inter—lux.

Horace.

LOUNGERS (in the phrase of Dr. Johnson), ' ambulatory students.'

Quis,   -   -   -
    -     -   -   - ut forte legentem,
Aut tacitum impellat, quovis sermone *molestus*.

Horace.

LOUNGERS are not only idle themselves, but the cause of idleness in others.   They are, literally, followers of that advice of the son of Sirach ; (See *Ecclus.* vi. 36.) ' If thou seest a man of understanding, get thee betimes to him, and *wear the steps of his door* '—For a further account of them, see ' *The Connoisseur,*'

* I take up a *lounging* book.

No. 82. *Letter to a young Gent. going to the University.* ' *The Guardian,*' *No.* 124. *Letter from Leo the Second, dated at his Den at*————*Cambridge;* and the ' *Spectator,*' *No.* 54. *Account of a New Sect of Philosophers which has arose in that famous Residence of Learning, the University of Cambridge.*

LOUNGING BOOK; a novel, or any book but a mathematical one. The late Mr. Maps, of Trumpington-street, possessed the most choice collection of LOUNGING BOOKS that the genius of Indolence could desire. The writer of these pages recollects seeing *Rabelais* in English; several copies of the *Reverend* Mr. Sterne's Tristram Shandy; Wycherly and Congreve's Plays; Joe Miller's Jests; Mrs. Behn's Novel's; and Lord Rochester's Poems, which are very *moving!* And to these we beg to add—The *Cambridge Tart,* and *Facetiæ Cantabrigienses.*

MALTING. Quaffing ' AUDIT' and other *Ales,* to speak à la Cantab, is termed *Malting.*

MANCIPLE. This office is obsolete. One who should *take in hand* to be tutor to the appetite. Horace insists that gentlemen who undertake this important office should be men of TASTE.

Nec sibi cænarum quivis temere arroget artem,
Non prius exacta tenui ratione *saporum.*

Sat. IV. Lib. II. 35.

MANDAMUS. A Special Mandate under the great seal, which enables a candidate to proceed to his degree before the regular period.

MAPPESIAN LIBRARY; founded by the late Mi. John Nicholson, alias *Maps,** of Trumpington-street. Mr. Maps, if Fame lie not, was originally, by profession, a *staymaker*, which, strange to relate, had not *attractions* sufficient to bind him to it long. He afterwards took to crying and hawking of *maps* about the several Colleges in the University, whence he acquired *all* his claim to eccentricity!!

MARSHAL. An officer who is generally engaged about the person of the Vice-chancellor, but on congregation days he attends in the lower house.

MASTER; the Head of a College; also Master of Arts.

Ingenium, sibi quod vacuas desumsit Athenas
Et studiis *annos septem* dedit—

> *Horace, Epist. III. L. II.*

We are told by T. Warton, in his History of English Poetry, that in the *Gesta Romanorum,* which was printed about the year 1479 (a copy of the second edition was in the possession of the late learned and ingenious Master of Emmanuel, Dr. Farmer), one of the magicians in it is styled ' MAGISTER peritus,' and sometimes Magister,† and that from the use of this word in the middle ages, the title MA-

---

*Mr. Maps' portrait, which now adorns the stair-case of the Public Library, was presented by the Undergraduates.

† If I mistake not, the same occurs in Reginald Scot's Discoverie of Witchcraft,—*quasi* Master of the *black* art. The following in Shakspeare has much puzzled the commentators : which, I do not doubt, has the same allusion. " Weak *musters* though ye be."—(*Tempest, Act 5.*)—' It is not easy,' says the author of the Revisal, ' to apprehend in what sense these aerial beings are called masters'—and proposes *ministers.*

GISTER in our Universities has its origin. Whatever they might have been formerly, *Masters of Arts*, in the present day, neither are, nor pretend to be, CONJURORS!

MASTER OF ARTS' COFFEE-HOUSE. It is sufficient to announce, that there is such a place, where M. A.'s meet together to take their coffee, *like other men!*—read the papers, and relate anecdotes of " the men of *our* College."

TO MATRICULATE. To enter the Student's name in the University Register. The following is from an occasional address spoken on Mr. Holman's first appearance at Covent Garden Theatre, Oct. 25th, 1784 :

> If you vouchsafe but to *matriculate*,
> And in the drama be his kind directors,
> No pupil e'er will more attend your lectures.

Mr. H. rose to very high *honours* in the school of Garrick.

MATRICULATION. The becoming an *actual* son of Alma Mater, by taking the oaths required by the University statutes, having previously subscribed your name in the Book of the Registracy.

M. B. A Bachelor of Physic must keep the greater part of nine several terms, and may be admitted any time in his sixth year. The exercises are one act and one opponency.

M. D. A Doctor of Physic is bound to the same regulations as L. L. D.

MUS. B. A Bachelor of Music must enter his name at some College, and compose and perform a solemn piece of Music as an exercise before the University.

MUS. D. A Doctor of Music is generally a Mus. B. and his exercise is the same.

MEDAL. Several gold Medals are annually given in the University of Cambridge to Students, whose classical and poetical compositions are deemed worthy of this distinction. These gentlemen are called Medallists.

There are also other Medals left by private benefactors to individual Colleges.

MEN.—Vix sunt HOMINES hoc nomine digni.
Ovid. de Trist.

At Cambridge, and eke at Oxford, every stripling is accounted a *Man* from the moment of his putting on the gown and cap. Consequently there are many MEN in our two Universities whose chins are out of all dread of a *lathering!*

TO MODERATE;—to perform the office of MoDERATOR in the schools. So Archbishop Usher, in a letter to Dr. Ward. 'They would needs impose upon me the MODERATING of the divinity act.' Again, in some encomiastic verses on Thomas Randolph, an ingenious poet:

When he in Cambridge schools did MODERATE,
Truth never found a subt'ler advocate.

MODERATOR; the President in the Schools. 'The hero, or principal character, of the drama, not much unlike the goddess *Victoria,* as described by the poets, hovering between two armies in an engagement, and with an arbitrary nod deciding the fate of the field. The MODERATOR struts between two wordy champions during the time of action, to see that they do not wander from the question in debate; and, when he perceives them deviating from it, to cut them short, and put them into the right road again.' *(Dr. Knox.)* See KEEP. The *moderators*

'cover their head,
'And, indede, they have nede, to kepe in theyr wyt.'

Hawkins's Old Plays.

NESCIO. "To *sport* a NESCIO;"—to shake the head, a signal that there is nothing in it. Strange and paradoxical as it may seem—to *sport* a NESCIO is very common with those who would, nevertheless, be thought very KNOWING.

NOBLEMEN.—By an interpretation of a statute made Jan. 31, 1577 the question, "how far the appellation of a *Nobleman* is to be extended?" it was decreed, that ' all are to be accounted for noble ; not only those who are barons, or superior to barons, in dignity; but also those who have any consanguinity, or affinity, to the royal Majesty. So as the title of the same dignity appertains to them *which*, as in our mother tongue we call, honourable personages, whether men, women, or *Maids of honour !!* For in such men and their sons, who shall seem to be next heirs to their parents, and otherwise shall be thought fit to adorn scholastical degrees, we think, that, not necessarily, nor strictly, the number of terms, nor the usual solemnity of ceremonies, or commencements, ought to be observed'(!!!) This statute is *strictly* observed. Lord Clarendon thought it ' an unhappy privilege which NOBLEMEN have, to choose whether they would be obliged to the public scholastic exercises— a *dishonorable* prerogative to be more ignorant than meaner men.' *(Dialogue concerning Education.)*— A Nobleman at the University might be described in the following lines of Horace.

Imberbus juvenis, tandem *custode** remoto :
Gaudet equis, canibus que, et *aprici gramine campi ;*†
Cereus in vitium flecti, *monitoribus asper,*‡
Utilium tardus provisor, *prodigus æris,*
Sublimis, cupidusque, et amata relinquere pernix.

NON ENS ; a Freshman in *Embryo!* one who has not been *matriculated,* though he has resided some time at the University, consequently is not considered as having any *being!*

NON PLACET. The term in which a *negative* vote is given in the Senate House.

NON READING MEN may be divided into several classes; there are loungers, dandies, bucks, bloods, Johns, Nimrods, and many others : quos nunc præscribere longum est.——

He was perfum'd like a milliner,
And 'twixt his finger and his thumb he held
A pouncet box, which ever and anon

---

* Tutor.   † Newmarket.   ‡ Master and Fellows.

He gave his nose, and still he smil'd and talk'd.
First Part Henry IV.

Fill high the sparkling bowl,
The rich repast prepare.
Gray's Bard.

Harry. Why, you're a high fellow Charles.

Goldfinch. To be sure! know the odds! hold four-in-hand—turn a corner in style—reins in form—elbows square, wrists pliant, hayait! drive the stage twice a week, pay for an inside place, mount the box, tip the coachee a crown, beat the mail, come in full speed, rattle down the gateway, take care of your head, never killed but one woman and a child in all my life—will you cut a card?—hide in the hat?—chuck in the glass?—draw cuts?—heads or tails?—gallop the maggot?—swim the hedge-hog?—any thing?—*Road to Ruin.*

NON TERM. When any Member of the Senate dies within the University during Term, on application to the Vice-chancellor, the University bell rings an hour; from which period *Non Term*, as to public lectures and disputations, commences for three days.

OPPONENT—(First, second, and third,) in keeping in the schools, those who begin the attack—
Make true or false, unjust or just,
Of no use but to be discuss'd:
Dispute and set a paradox
Like a strait boot upon the stocks.
Hud.

Ne Hercules contra duos, says the proverb. It often

happens, however, that the *Act*, or *Respondent*, is an hyper-Hercules, and more than a match for the *three*. —The skill of the *Opponents* consists in making

> 'the worse appear
> The better reason—to perplex, and *dash*—(qu.
> *Dish?* See "*dish*.")
> Maturest counsels.'   *Milton, P. L.*

OPTIME SENIOR. The title of those who obtain the second rank in the Mathematical Tripos. Quibus sua reservatur senioritas in comitiis *prioribus*, who formerly ranked with Wranglers.

OPTIME JUNIOR. The last honours of the Tripos list. Those quibus sua reservatur senioritas in comitiis *posterioribus*.

ORATOR. Public, is the voice of the Senate on all public occasions; writes, reads, and records the letters to and from the body of the Senate, and presents to all honorary degrees with an appropriate speech. This is esteemed one of the most honourable offices in the gift of the University.

PENSIONERS; the same with *Commoners* at Oxford; a rank of Students between Fellow Commoners and above Sizers. 'A Pensioner is generally a person of genteel fortune, and good expectancy, who wishes to pass through the usual routine of collegiate exercises without any pecuniary emolument, without enviable distinctions, or singular obsequiousness.' *Gent. Mag. Vol. LXV. p.* 20. If by "pecuniary emolument" is meant *exhibitions* from the College, or from other corporate bodies, this statement is not correct. The number of *Pensioners* is very considerable, who would be obliged to change their gown for a *Sizer's*, were it not for the pecuniary assistance they receive from city exhibitions, &c. which are seldom obtained without "singular obsequiousness," and the most mortifying servility.

PIECE; a plat of ground adjoining the College; as, Pembroke *Piece,* &c. Also a PIECE; one who is well acquainted with PROPRIA QUÆ MARIBUS. "Plutarch reckons up the names of some elegant PIECES, Leontia, Boedina, Hedicia, Nicedia, that were frequently seen in Epicurus' garden." (*Burton's Anatomy of Melancholy, Edit.* 1682. *fol. P.* ii. §. 2. *p.* 280.)

PIT; the place of St. Mary's reserved for the accommodation of Masters of Arts, and *Fellow Commoners.* The latter are

"In PIT superlatively fine."
Imit. of Horace.

The Noblemen sit in GOLGOTHA. The Bachelors of Arts mix promiscuously with the Undergraduates, in the gallery. The *Proctors* sit in the *Pit,* and make a very awful appearance.

PLACET. The term in which an *affirmative* vote is given in the Senate House.

TO BE PLUCK'D; to be, in the fashionable *cant* phrase—*done up*—DISH'D to all intents and purposes

—to be refused a degree or orders for the church, through insufficiency.

Epigram on a Cantab who was pluck'd for orders.

Ned cut off his queue, and was powder'd with care,
    Yet sadly mistaken was Ned,
For tho' he had taken such pains with his *hair,*
    The Bishop found fault with his *head.*

" Mr. Scurlock, A. B. Fellow of Jesus College (Oxford), was PLUCK'D, (i. e. *disgraced,* and *forbade to proceed in performing his exercise,)* for mentioning the word KING in his declamation."

                    (Terræ Filius, No. 50.)

Tempora mutantur. God bless his present *Majesty* George IV. chorus of Cantabs. ' AMEN'

PONS ASINORUM (vide Asses' Bridge.)

POLLOI, οι πολλοι, "the many." Those who take their degree without any honour.

" Οι πολλοι," says Dr. Bentley, " is a known expression in profane authors, opposed *sometimes* τοις σοφοις, *to the wise,* and ever denotes the most, and generally the meanest, of mankind." *(Sermon preached before the University of Cambridge, Nov. 5, 1715.)*

The following ' Ode to the unambitious and *undistinguished* Bachelors,' is not, like the subject of it, destitute of *merit.*

        Post tot naufragia tutus.

              G

"Thrice happy ye, through toil and dangers past,
  Who rest upon that peaceful shore,
  Where all your fagging is no more,
And gain the long-expected port at last.

Yours are the sweet, the ravishing delights,
  To doze and snore upon your noon-tide beds:
No chapel-bell your peaceful sleep affrights,
  No problems trouble now your empty heads:
Yet, if the heav'nly Muse is not mistaken,
  And poets say the Muse can rightly guess;
  I fear, full many of you must confess,
That ye have barely *sav'd your bacon.*

Amidst the problematic war,
  Where dire equations frown in dread array;
  Ye never strove to find the arduous way,
To where proud GRANTA's honours shine afar.
  Within that dreadful mansion have ye stood,
Where MODERATORS glare with looks uncivil,
  How often have ye d—d their souls, their blood,
And wish'd all mathematics at the d——l!

But ah! what terrors, on that fatal day,
  Your souls appall'd, when, to your stupid gaze,
  Appear'd the bi-quadratic's darken'd maze,
And problems rang'd in horrible array!

Hard was the task, I ween, the labour great,
  To the wish'd port to find your uncouth way—
How did ye toil, and fag, and fume, and fret,
  And —— what the bashful Muse would blush to say.

But now your painful tremors all are o'er—
  Cloth'd in the glories of a full sleev'd gown,
  Ye strut majestically up and down,
And now ye fag, and now ye fear no more."

PRÆLECTOR, or Father of the College (quod vide).

PRESIDENT. The Master of Queen's College— In St. John's, Caius, Pembroke, Magdalen, and Catherine Colleges, the next in rank to the Master is so called, which answers to the Vice-master in Trinity, &c. &c.

PRIZEMEN. 'Palmam qui meruit ferat.' There are various prizes given to Members of the University, who have distinguished themselves, which in some instances consist of *ponderous* folios. Dr. Johnson would not have felt the full force of such an *overwhelming* compliment, as the worthy Lexicographer considered a great book a great evil, 'μεγα βιβλον μεγα κακον. Such also was the opinion of the late Duke of Cumberland, who, when Gibbon triumphantly presented the last volume of his Roman Empire to his Royal Highness, exclaimed, to the no small mortification of the historian, " What another d—d big book Mr. Gibbon? hey!"

See Davis's Bibliographical Olio.

*PROCTOR, an academical officer,whose business

---

* The Proctors are also required to be present at all congregations of the Senate, to take the suffrages of the house, to read the Graces in the regent house, to take secretly the assent or dissent, and openly pronounce the same. They must be M. A.'s of at least two years' standing; but of whatever standing, are Regents by virtue of their office. (*Ed.*)

it is, * περιπολεισθαι, to *walk the round,* and see that there is no chambering and wantonness, no rioting and drunkenness. PROCTORS had need be Masters of ARTS, for they are exposed to many *scrapes.*

PROCTOR'S MEN (alias Bull dogs, quod vide). Not Gog nor Magog are more fierce in their exterior. They accompany the Proctor on all public occasions, carrying the University statutes, and in all his dangerous enterprises, enforcing his orders with an *irresistible* dexterity.—Deprendi miserum est. *Horace.*

PROFESSOR. There are five Regius Professorships, and many others founded by various benefactors. The possessors of which give lectures on the various branches of divinity, science, &c. during term.

PROPROCTORS. These officers were appointed in consequence of the increasing magnitude of the University, to assist the Proctors in that part of their duty which relates to the discipline and behaviour of those who are in *statu pupillari,* and the preservation of public morals.

TO PROSE; to tire with prolixity. " Of the three *opponents,* he mentioned one who, in his opinion, PROSED very much in explaining the arguments." *(Gent. Mag.)*—Also, to PROSE, to 'sit with a sad, leaden, downward cast.' (See *Milton's Il Penseroso; or, Poem in Praise of Prosing;)* to be wholly absorbed in thought. Mathematical men have been addicted to PROSING from the time of Archimedes, who, as is well known, caught his death by a fit of it.—(See *Plu-*

* Qu. περιπατεισθαι. *Printer's Devil.*

Quite Unexpected.

tarch.)—It is related, likewise, by Stobæus, that the servants of this wonderful man were accustomed, at bathing times, to take him by force from the table, where he drew mathematical figures with such a fixed attention, that he continued to draw them on his anointed body; *not knowing where he was,* while his servants were pouring ointments upon him, and preparing him for the bath.

PROSER. 'One who, while you fancy he is admiring a beautiful woman, it is an even wager that he is solving a proposition in Euclid.' *(Spect. No. 77.)* —Chaucer's clerk in astronomy was an arrant, or *errant* PROSER.

> He walked into the feldes for to pry
> Upon the sterre, to wete what should befall;
> Til he was in a marl pit yfall—
> He saw not that.

Miller's Tale.—Edit. by Speght, 1598.

PROVOST. The title appropriated, solely, to the President of King's College. 'On the choice of a *Provost,*' says the author of a History of the University of Cambridge, 1753, ' the Fellows are all shut into the anti-chapel, *and* out of which they are not permitted to stir on any account, nor *none* permitted to enter, till they have all agreed on their *man;* which agreement sometimes takes up several days; and, if I remember right, they were three days and nights confined in choosing the present *Provost,* and had their beds, CLOSE-STOOLS, &c. with them, and their commons, &c. given them in at the windows.'—One does not see what occasion they could have for CLOSE-STOOLS, being so HARD BOUND!

PUNISHMENT. We *now* use this to signify nothing more than an *imposition* (see IMPOSITION); and, the being enjoined to *get the first book of the Iliad by heart,* would be thought a severe "*punishment.*" It may be worth while, however, to see, in what *sense* the word was used in the more *barbarous* ages, as they are very properly called. From the following verses of Milton—

Nec duri libet usque minas perferre magistri,
Cæteraque ingenio, non subeunda, meo—

It has been taken for granted, that he suffered *flagellation* at Cambridge. The late Reverend and learned Thomas Warton, adopting 'apt alliteration's artful aid,' affirms, that 'in those days of *simplicity* and *subordination,* of *roughness* and *rigour,* this sort of punishment was much more *common,* and *consequently,* by no means so disgraceful for a young man at the University as it would be thought at present.' After Warton, the testimony of Samuel Johnson is deserving attention. The Doctor, who has LASH'D Milton most unmercifully with his *pen* (see his *Life*), yet tenderly and delicately says, alluding to the POSTERIORI evidence, 'I am ashamed to relate, what I *fear* is true, that Milton was the last student in either University that suffered the public indignity of corporal punishment.' The officer who bore the *fasces,* and performed this FUNDAMENTAL part of discipline, was Dr. Thomas Bainbrigge, Master of Christ's College. The same punishment was introduced in domestic

education. ' Fathers and mothers,' says Aubrey, ' used
to *lash* their daughters when they were perfect women.'
Proh pudor!—A school-master, who undertook to
translate Horace, rendered the following ;

sublimi flagello
Tange Chloen semel arrogantem.

On scornful Chloe lift thy wand,
And SCOURGE her with *unpitying* hand. (!!!)

In Sir John Fenn's Collection of Letters, written
during the reign of Henry VI., &c. we find one of the
GENTLE SEX prescribing for her son, who was at
Cambridge, as follows :—

- - - " prey (i. e. entreat) Grenefield to send me faith-
fully worde by wrytyn, who (how) Clemit Paston
hathe do his dever i' lernyng (done his endeavour in
learning), and if he hathe nought do (done) well, nor
wyll nought amend, prey hym that he wyll trewly
BELASCH hym* tyl he wyll amend, and so ded (did)
the last maystr, and yᵉ best, eu' (ever) he had att
Caumbrege."

The GENTLE-woman concludes with a promise to
give Master Grenefield " X m'rs" i. e. *ten marks,* for
his pains ! We do not learn how many MARKS young
Master Clement received ; who, certainly, *took* more
pains, though of another nature—PATIENDO non *fa-
ciendo*—FERENDO non *feriendo*.

An old poet, Thomas Tusser, author of Five Hun-

---

* *Trewly* BELASCH him —IN *plain* English—*give him a* GOOD, HEARTY
FLOGGING.

dred points of good Husbandry, thus piteously com-
plains of the treatment he met with in his " boyish
days:"

> From Paul's I went, to Eton sent,
> To learn straight-ways the Latin phrase,
> Where *fifty-three* stripes giv'n to me,
> At once I had:
> For fault but small, or none at all,
> It came to pass thus beat I *was*,
> See, UDALL,* see, the mercy of thee,
> To me poor lad!

We are happy to state, as an instance of superior
refinement and civilization in the present age, that
this mode of correction, which is very *cutting* to a man
of the least *sense* or *feeling*, is almost obsolete in our
public schools. Of its specific virtue, however, no
doubt was entertained by our forefathers; and the
name of BUSBY will be long remembered, for his vi-
gorous and determined perseverance in going to the
very BOTTOM in discipline. Other men have arisen
to fame by the happy strokes of their *pen;* he, by the
less happy, but more *lively*, more *feeling*, more *home*
strokes of his ROD! No man ever afforded a more
striking illustration of that old saying, ARS *patet*
omnibus, than he did; and with equal truth it might
be said, that no master ever gave his scholars more
reason to *remember* him.

---

* It is said, that this *Udall* was the first man that King James the First
inquired for when he came to England; and, hearing of his decease, exclaimed, ' By my sal, then, the greatest scholar in Europe's dead!'

In the statutes of Trinity College, An. 1556, the scholars of the foundation are ordered to be *whipp'd* even to the twentieth year. ' Dr. Potter,' says Aubrey, ' while a Tutor of Trinity College (Oxford), *whipt* his pupil *with his sword by his side* when he came to take his leave of him to go to the inns of court.' This was done to make him a *smart* fellow !

QUESTIONIST. One who has been

> ' long tow'rds mathematics,
> Optics, philosophy, and statics.'
>
> *Hud.*

SOPHS of the highest order ; also men who have passed their examinations, and are admitted ad respondendum quæstioni.

QUIZ.—This word is used in a variety of senses. (1.) In a good sense. *One who will not be shamed out of his virtue, nor laughed out of his innocency.* Hence the punning quotation—VIR BONUS EST QUIZ. There were *Quizzes* of this description in the primitive ages. See Wisdom of Solomon, II. 15, &c. Such kind of *quizzicalness* cannot be better recommended than in the words of a writer who has been too much neglected—honest old Jeremy Collier. (See his ingenious ESSAYS.)—" Arm yourself with recollection, and be always on your guard : make a strong resolution in your defence ; *that* goes a great way in most cases. Have a care of a weak complaisance, and of being *preposterously* GOOD NATURED, as they call it—you'll pardon the expression. Be not overborne by importunity :—never surrender to a jest, nor make the company master of your conscience. Venture to be so morose (i. e. *quizzical*) as to maintain the reason of a man, and the innocence of a Christian. 'Tis no disgrace to be healthy in a common infection. *Singularity in* VIRTUE, *and* DISCRETION, *is a commendation, I take it."—(Essay on Drunkenness.**)*

By a *Quiz* is commonly understood, in the words of Ben Jonson, ' one who affects the violence of Singularity in *all* he does.' (Here a little well-tempered ridicule may be of service—) In defining a QUIZ, adde VULTUM, HABITUMQUE hominis, as Horace says. And first, for his physiognomy. ' It is impossible to account for the persecution of these beings (QUIZZES), unless we suppose, that non-resistance only sharpens that rage, which UGLINESS originally provoked.' (The Microcosm.)—Adde *habitum*. In the second place, a man sometimes obtains the odious appellation of a QUIZ merely from his stile of *dressing;* which is, *ex pede*, different from orthodox, or established fashion.

> *Rideri* possit, eo quod
> *Rusticius* tonso *toga* defluit, et male laxus
> In pede calceus hæret.   -   -   -   -
> -   -   at est *bonus*, ut melior vir
> Non alius quisquam; at tibi amicus : At *Ingenium ingens*
> *Inculto latet hoc sub corpore.*
> > ***Horace.***

Still, for all that, he is a QUIZ !

---

* The being enjoined to turn a page, or two, of this Essay *into Latin*, would be a much more useful IMPOSITION on account of any irregularity, than the being appointed to get by heart " two or three hundred rumblers out of Homer, in commendation of Achilles' toes, or the Grecian's boots."
(*Archdeacon Echard's Contempt of the Clergy.*)

The most borish of all *quizzes* is, however, the
Laudator temporis acti, Se puero. " Oh the days
when I was young."

RAFF (probably contracted from Rag-a-muf-
fin); a dirty, low, vulgar fellow; one whose vices
are not the vices of *a gentleman.*

TO READ (a very emphatical word); the same
with Fag.—" To read for an honour." *(Phrase.)*

A READING-MAN; one whose mind is devoted
to nothing else but the study of the Mathematics:
one who, though naturally, perhaps, of a peaceable,
quiet temper, and disposition, so congenial to study,
yet whose highest ambition is to be accounted the
greatest wrangler in the University!

> " Hence, loathed Mathematics!
>   Of lecturer and blackest tutor born,
>   In lecture-room forlorn,
> 'Mongst horrid quizzes, bloods, and bucks unholy;
>   Find out some uncouth cell,
> Where pallid Study spreads his midnight wings,
>   And dismal ditties sings;
> There, midst unhallow'd souls, with sapless brain,
>   Compose thy sober train,
> And in the mind of reading Quizzes dwell."

The following quotations admirably define the
character of this class of men:

These self-devoted from the prime of youth,
To life sequester'd, and ascetic truth.—*Harte.*

In garrets dark he smokes and puns,
A prey to discipline and duns,
And now intent on new designs,
Sighs for a fellowship and fines.

Progress of Discontent.

REDEAT. It is the custom in some Colleges, on coming into residence, to wait on the Dean, and sign your name in a book, kept for that purpose, which is called signing your *Redeat.*

REGENTS; Masters of Arts under five years standing in the University; who are appointed, by Statute, *Regere in Artibus,* i. e. to preside in the School of Arts during that time.—Egregii viri, vindicate protestatem vestram; memineritis vos non frustra Magistrorum et REGENTIUM nomine insigniri. *Dean Bathurst.—(Orat. habit in dom. convoc. Oxon.)*

NON REGENTS; those whose Regency has ceased by being above five years standing. A Non Regent's hood is entirely of black silk.—The terms REGENT and NON REGENT are as old as the reign of Edward the Sixth.

REGISTRARY. This officer is obliged, either by himself or deputy properly authorized, to attend all Congregations, to give directions, if it be required, for the due form of such graces as are to be propounded, to receive them when passed in both Houses, and to register them in the University records. To register also the Seniority of such as proceed yearly in any of the arts and faculties, according to the schedules delivered unto him by the Proctors.

RESPONDENT; the same with ACT.

RETRO: a *behind*-hand accompt. A cook's bill of extraordinaries not settled by the Tutor.

A ROW; a riot—To ROW a room; to break the furniture. This is not uncommon after a wine party, when BACCHUS, the APOLLO *Virorum, (Cantabrig.)* has taken possession of the *head* quarters, and Reason is obliged to surrender.

RUSTICATION. " It seems plain from his own verses to Diodati, that Milton had incurred RUSTICATION—*a temporary dismission into the country, with, perhaps, the loss of a term.*"—(Dr. Johnson.) It is, sometimes, with the loss of *a year:* i. e. *three* terms. The next sentence to RUSTICATION, is EXPULSION, when the unhappy Student may exclaim, *Farewell,* FOR EVER, *to all my former greatness!* This (latter) one would, in common candour, suppose had never been enforced, but upon some great and CRYING occasion. Yet Sergeant Miller, in his Account of the University of Cambridge, relates, that " Dr. Bentley, without any summons, proof, or ceremony, or even the consent of the senior Fellows, expelled one HANSON, a poor *subsizer,* for what in general terms he calls, a foul and scandalous offence: though at Ely House he endeavoured to prove it was for going to a Presbyterian Meeting."!! Excessive sanctity is an *offence* which is never complained of, in the present day, either at Cambridge, or Oxford.

The following Verses, entitled, " The *Rusticated* Cantab," appeared in the Morning Herald :

Dread worthies, I bow at your shrine,
   And, kneeling submissive, petition
You'll pardon this false step of mine,
   And pity my dismal condition.

When ye met altogether of late,
   In the room which we term COMBINATION,
To fix your petitioner's fate,
   Alas! why do you chuse RUSTICATION ?

That my conduct was wrong I must own,
   And your justice am forc'd to acknowledge;
But can I in no wise atone
   For my fault, without leaving the College ?

Consider how strange 'twill appear,
   In the mind of each fine jolly Fellow,
That a Cantab was *banish'd a year*,
   Just for *roving* a little when mellow.

You have precedents, no one denies,
   To prove it but just that I went hence;
But surely no harm could arise,
   If you were to relax in your sentence.

No, trust me, much good should proceed
   From granting this very great favour;
For, impress'd with a sense of the deed,
   I'd carefully mend my behaviour.

D.D.   Esqr. Bedell.   Mus.D.   D.D.   Nobleman.   D.D.   L.L.D.   M.D.

In Surplice.   In Congregaton. Robe.   State Robe.   Scarlet Robe.   Congregation Robe.

You will then have on me a strong hold,
   For Gratitude's stronger than any tie :
Then pray do not think me too bold,
   In thus begging hard for some lenity !

But why should I humbly implore,
   Since to you all my sorrow's a farce ?
I'll supplicate Fellows no more ;
   So, ye reverend Dons, *caret pars.*

SAINTS. " A set of men who have great preten-
sions to particular sanctity of manners, and zeal for
*orthodoxy." *(See proceedings against W. Frend,
M. A. published by himself.)*

SATIS; the lowest honour in the Schools. *Satis
disputasti;* which is as much as to say, in the colloquial stile, " Bad enough."—*Satis et bene disputasti.* Pretty fair—Tolerable.—Satis, et *optime* disputasti, *Go thy ways, thou flower and quintessence
of* WRANGLERS ! Such are the compliments to be
expected from the Moderator, after the *act* is kept.

SCARLET DAYS. Certain Festivals in the Church
of England, upon which the Doctors in the three
learned professions appear in their Scarlet Robes.
Noblemen also residing in the Universities wear their
full dresses on these occasions.

SCHOLARS. Those Students who have obtained
by their erudition, certain emoluments, arising from
benefactions left for the purpose of founding *Scholar-*

* The modern Saints are much more inclined to heterodoxy ; and indeed
appear to wish to undermine the foundations of the Protestant Established
Church.—" Scatter our Enemies."—National Song.

ships. The majority of which are confined to particular Colleges ; but the most honourable are open to
competion of the whole University.

TO SCONCE; to impose a fine. *(Academical
Phrase.) Grose's Dict.* This word is, I believe,
wholly confined to Oxford.——" A young Fellow
of Baliol College, having, upon some discontent,
cut his throat very dangerously, the Master of the
College sent his servitor to the buttery-book to SCONCE
(i. e. fine) him 5*s.*; and, says the Doctor, Tell him the
next time he cuts his throat, I'll *sconce* him *ten.*"
(Terræ Filius, No. 39.*)*

SCRAPING ; shuffling of the feet.—This is practised at St. Mary's, and is no *tacit* mark of disap-
probation of the preacher, or of his doctrine, or of
the length of his discourse. The late Gilbert Wakefield scruples not to confess, in his 'Memoirs,' that
he was too prone to mischiefs of this nature, p. 3.
SCRAPING seems to have been of great antiquity.
In one of Hugh Latimer's sermons, preached before
King Edward the Sixth, is the following passage :

" Et loquentem eum audierunt in silentio, et seriem
lectionis non interrumpentes." 'They heard him,'
saith he (Chrysostom), ' in silence; not interrupting
the order of his preaching.' " He meanes, they heard
him quietly, without any SHOVELING feete." *(Fruitful
Sermons,* 4*to.* 1635. *B. L.*)

SCRIBBLING PAPER; an inferior sort used by
the mathematicians, and in the lecture room. The

ancient mathematicians used to draw their figures on the sand—*exarantur illæ figuræ, ac lineæ in pulvere*—by which means they avoided the inconveniency of blotting—*Ut si quid rectum non sit, facile corrigatur.*

SCRUTATORS; these officers are Non Regents, whose duty it is to attend all congregations, to read the graces in the lower house, to gather all votes secretly, or take them openly in scrutiny, and publicly to pronounce the assent or dissent of that house.

SENATE HOUSE. Within the sacred walls of this edifice, the sons of GRANTA generally undergo their final examination, previously to their being admitted to the degree of A. B. Here also are conferred all other degrees; and Congregations are held to transact and regulate the special affairs of the University.

> Here education, power divine,
>   Her favourite temple long has plann'd,
> And calls around her sacred shrine
>   To guard her laws a chosen band.
> Conducts each dubious step by reason's plan,
> Nor tamely yields the sacred rights of man.
> *Roscoe.*

> Go soar with Plato to the empyreal sphere,
> To the first good, first perfect, and first fair.
> *Pope.*

> How charming is divine Philosophy,
> Not harsh and crabbed, as dull fools suppose,
> But musical, as is Apollo's lyre,
> And a perpetual feast of nectar'd sweets,
> Where no crude surfeit reigns.
> *Milton.*

H

SIMEONITES ;—(A correspondent to the Gent. Mag. asks, and has not been answered, ' Why the inhabitants of *Magdalene College continue to be styled SIMEONITES?' disciples and followers of the reverend and *pious* Charles Simeon, M. A. Fellow of King's College—inventor of) " SKELETONS of Sermon's !!" &c. &c. &c.

SIZE—*in academiis*, from *Assise*—Fr. *Asseoir*, to set down, sc. *sumptus qui in tabulas referuntur.* Ray derives it from *scindo.* Minshew has inserted the word in his Guide into Tongues, second Ed. 1626, and with it, the following. " A SIZE is a portion of bread and drinke; it is a *farthing*, which schollers in Cambridge have at the buttery; it is noted with the letter S. as in Oxford with the letter Q. for halfe a farthing; and whereas they say in Oxford, to *battle* in the Buttery-booke, i. e. to set downe on their names what they take in bread, drinke, butter, cheese, &c.; so in CAMBRIDGE, they say, to SIZE, i. e. to set downe their *quantum*, i. e. how much they take on their name in the Buttery-booke." This word, as was observed of EXHIBITION, was not confined to the University. King Lear, in Shakspear's inimitable Tragedy, is made to address one of his daughters ;

'Tis not in thee
To grudge my pleasure, to cut off my train,
To bandy hasty words, to scant my SIZES.—

TO SIZE, " at dinner, is to order yourself any little luxury that may chance to tempt you, in ad-

---

* Together with the rage for tea, and other harmless potations. The Queen's men have *imbibed* the doctrines of the *apostolic Simeon.* In their Vocabulary—Bene Potus is no longer a four bottle Man, but one who has discussed his seventh cup of Souchong.

dition to your general fare; for which you are expected
to pay the cook at the end of the term." This is
often done when the *commons* are scanty or indifferent.
As a College term, it is of very considerable antiquity.
In the Comedy called ' The Return from Parnassus,
1606,' one of the characters says,

' You that are one of the Devil's FELLOW COM-
MONERS; one that SIZETH the Devil's *butteries;*
one that are so dear to Lucifer, that he never puts
you out of *Commons* for non-payment,' &c.

Again in the same; 'Fidlers, I use to *size* my
music, or go on the *score* for it.'

*SIZAR, or SIZER; ' *equivalent* to *Servitor* at
Oxford, and is commonly a young man of *mean* and
poor extraction, and one who comes to College to
mend his circumstances, and to gain a *comfortable
livelihood* by means of his literary acquirements.'
(*Gent. Mag.*)—Not one word of this is true! Yet,
in all the Dictionaries, Johnson's not excepted,
SIZER is said to be the same with " *equivalent*," or
answering to, SERVITOR. Whoever has resided any
little time at Cambridge, must know, that, in point of
rank, the distinction between *Pensioners* and *Sizers*
is by no means considerable. Between *Commoners*
and *Servitors* there is a great gulf fixed. Nothing is
more common, than to see *Pensioners* and *Sizers*
taking sweet counsel together, and walking arm in
arm, to St. Mary's, as friends.† Formerly, indeed,
the *Sizers* were required to wait at table; but this
painful and disgraceful injunction is abolished; in

ʳ Subsizer was also formerly used, but we believe is now exploded.
(Vide Miller's University of Cambridge.)

† The Sizers occupy the same seats as the Pensioners.

consequence of which, many very respectable, though not opulent, families are not ashamed to enter their sons of this rank of Students. The *Sizers* are allowed their *Commons* in Hall; Eustatius remarks, it was accounted a great favour in the Emperour's granting any learned man—εν Μουσεια σιτησιν, i. e. his *College Sizings.*—With respect to their going to the University to *mend their circumstances,* I only answer, *would it were so!* In addition to City Exhibitions, and College allowances, no small income is required to maintain even a SIZER, in these times, with decency. —(*See Enormous Expense in Education at the University of Cambridge,* 8*vo.* 1788.) In respect to their academical habit: At Trinity and St. John's Colleges, the *Sizers* wear precisely the same dress with the Pensioners. At other Colleges, the only difference is, that their gowns are not bordered with velvet.* At Peter-House, the *Pensioner's* gown is the same as is worn by the Bachelors of Arts; and the *Sizers'* is the same as is worn by the *Pensioners* of St. John's, Emmanuel, &c. In every College, the *Sizers* invite, and are invited by, the *Pensioners* to wine parties; and some of them (the former) endeavour to vie with the latter in fashionable frivolity. Alluding to the ancient custom of compelling them to wait at the Fellows' table, Kit Smart, a son of genius, thus humorously alludes in his *Tripos* on *Yawning.*

Haud aliter Socium esuriens SIZATOR edacem
Dum videt, appositusque cibus frustratur hiantem,
Dentibus infundens, nequicquam brachia tendit,
Sedulus officiosa dapes removere paratus.—

* The Sizers now, on becoming Scholars, at most of the Colleges sport velvet.'

SIZINGS. Little delicacies which men have the privilege of ordering—and paying for. To be put out of Sizings, i. e. to be refused this privilege, is therefore no uncommon punishment.

SIZING BELL; a bell which is rung every evening, at eight o'clock, to signify that the *Sizing Bill* is ready. *(obsolete.)*

SIZING PARTY differs from a supper in this; viz. at a *Sizing Party* every one of the guests contributes his *part;* i. e. orders what he pleases, at his own expense, to his friend's rooms. "A *part* of fowl," or duck; a roasted pigeon; "a *part* of apple pye." These *Sizing Parties* remind us of Homer's δαιτα εισην, as explained by *Madam* Dacier. A sober *beaker* of brandy, or rum, or hollands and water, concludes the entertainment. In our days, a bowl of Bishop, or milk punch, with a chaunt, generally winds up the carousal.

SNOBS. A term applied indiscriminately to all who have not the honour of being Members of the University; but in a more particular manner to the '*profanum Vulgus*,' the Tag-rag, and Bobtail, who vegetate on the sedgy banks of Camus; and who appear to have a natural antipathy to the '*Gens Togata.*'

SOPHS. Senior Sophs, or Sophisters; Students in their last year.

SOPHISH GOWN; one that bears the marks of having seen a great deal of service;—"a thing of shreds and patches." So in the old Comedy of *The Poor Scholar,*—speaking of certain SOPHS of this description;

> Their *old rags* are badges of honour :
> A coat of arms, the older 'tis and plainer,
> 'Tis the more honourable: their *habit* does
> Declare unto the world, that they have been
> In hot and furious skirmishes, they are so
> Slasht and cut.

SOPH-MOR; ' the next distinctive appellation to Freshman.' A writer in the Gent. Mag. thinks MOR ' an abbreviation of the Greek Μοϱια, introduced at a time when the *Encomium Moriæ,* the Praise of Folly, of Erasmus, was so generally used.' This is a most surprising conjecture !

SPINNING HOUSE; an ergastulum; a house of labour and correction; a prison for prostitutes under the jurisdiction of the Vice-chancellor and Proctors. Those of whom they take cognizance, are *omnes pronubas meretrices et mulieres incontinentes notabiliter delinquentes.*

> Millions of such creatures walk the earth
> *Obscene,* both when we wake, and when we sleep.

SPOON. The last of each class of the honours is denominated *The Spoon.* Thus the last Wrangler is called the Golden Spoon—the last Senior Optime the Silver Spoon—and the last Junior Optime the Wooden Spoon. The Wooden Spoon, however, is εκαθ ξοχην. ' The Spoon.' This invidious distinction sticks to a man through life. (*Vide Cambridge Tart, pages* 98 *and* 284.)

TO SPORT. A word *sacred* to men of fashion. Whatever they do, is nothing but sporting. 'One man *sports* a paradoxical walking-stick.' *(Grose's Olio.)*—(or piece of plant.)—Another *sports* his beaver* at noon-day—*sports* his dog, and his gun—*sports* his shooting-jacket.—"With regard to the word SPORT, they (the Cantabrigians) *sported* knowing, and they *sported* ignorant—they *sported* an *Egrotat*, and they *sported* a new Coat—they *sported* an *Exeat;* they *sported* a *Dormiat*, &c."—*(Gent. Mag. Dec.* 1794.*)*

TO SPORT A DOOR; to break it open.† "To break the windows of a College, to disturb a peaceable Student by what is called SPORTING his door at midnight, &c. these are the methods which young men of spirit have often adopted to display their fire." *(Dr. Knox.)*—The practice is very ancient.

> Non est flagitium—adolescentulum
>   –   –   –   –   –   *fores*
> *Effringere.*
>   *Ter. Adelph. A.* **1.** *Sc.* **2.**

A SPORTING MAN; a *dashing* fellow; a *statute breaker*; a Newmarket *lounger;* one who asks himself, with Chaucer,

> Whereto should I study, and make myself wood,
>   (i. e. *mad;)*
> Upon a booke alway in cloister to pore ?
>   *Prolog. to the Monke.*

---

* Scilicet Hat, vice Cloth—Cap.

† The acceptation of this word is now entirely different, as ' to sport *oak*, or a door, is, in the modern phrase, to exclude *duns*, or other unpleasant intruders.

Horace very finely alludes to a *sporting man*, in the following :

> Hunc si perconteris, avi cur atque parentis
> Præclaram ingrata stringat malus ingluvie rem,
> Omnia conductis comens obsonia nummis?
> Sordidus, *atque animi quod parvi* nolit haberi.
>
> Sat. II. Lib. I. v. 7.

Quasi, Quiz. The following 'Song' was written by a gentleman of *sporting* talents, and appeared in the Morning Chronicle. The latter part would be more agreeable, if there was more *levity* in it. The author sports *serious*, which is out of character!

Come, ye good College lads, and attend to my lays,
   I'll shew you the folly of poring o'er books;
For all ye get by it is mere empty praise,
   Or a poor meagre fellowship, and sallow looks.

Chorus.

Then lay by your books, lads, and never repine;
     And cram not your attics
     With dry mathematics,
But moisten your clay with a bumper of wine.

The first of mechanics was old Archimedes,
   Who play'd with Rome's ships, as he'd play cup
     and ball;
To play the same game, I can't see where the need is—
   Or why we should fag mathematics at all!

   Chorus.—Then lay by your books, lads, &c.

Great Newton found out the Binomial law,
   To raise x + y to the power of b;

Found the distance of planets that he never saw,
   And which we most probably never shall see.

   Chorus.—Then lay by your books, lads, &c.

Let Whiston and Ditton* star-gazing enjoy,
   And taste all the sweets mathematics can give ;
Let us for our time find out better employ,
   And knowing life's sweets, let us learn how to *live.*

   Chorus.—Then lay by your books, lads, &c.

These men *ex absurdo* conclusions may draw ;
   Perpetual motion they never could find :
Not one of the set, lads, could balance a straw—
   And longitude-seeking is hunting the wind.

   Chorus.—Then lay by your books, lads, &c.

If we study at all, let us study the means
   To make ourselves friends, and to keep them when
      made ;
Learn to value the blessings kind Heaven ordains—
   To make other men happy, let that be our trade.

          Chorus.

Let each day be better than each day before ;
      Without pain or sorrow,
      To-day or to-morrow,
May we live, my good lads, to see many days more.

SPREAD ; a feast of a more humble description
than a *Gaudy,* (quod vide) and generally consisting

* It was on the heads of these learned astronomers, that Swift discharged
his celebrated and savoury stanza :

    ' Let Whiston and Ditton,' &c. &c.

of cold fowls, sauce, &c. sufficient to keep body and soul together.

STANDING; academical age, or rank. " Of what *standing* are you? I am a *Senior* SOPH." To *stand* for an honour. (Phr.)—The learned Godwyn supposes, that ' the juridical phrases among the Romans —STARE *in senatu,* to prevail in the senate; Causâ cadere, to be cast in one's suit; have been taken out of their Fencing-schools, where the set posture of the body, by which a man prepares himself to fight and grapple with the enemy, is termed *Status* or *Gradus.* As *cedere de statu* to give back—*Gradum vel statum servare,* to keep one's *standing*—And that from thence those elegancies have been translated into places of judgment.'

S. T. B. Sanctæ Theologiæ Baccalaureus, vide B. D.

S. T. P. Sanctæ Theologiæ Professor, vide D. D.

STUDENT; a member of the University, in statu pupillari.—Qu. *Student* a non studendo—as Lucus a non lucendo.

SUPPLICAT; an entreaty to be admitted to the degree of A. B.; containing a certificate that the Questionist has kept his full number of terms, or explaining any deficiency. This document is presented to the caput by the father of his college.

SURPLICE DAYS; on all Sundays, and Saint-days, and the evenings preceding, every member of the University, except noblemen, attend chapel in their surplices.

SYNDICS ; certain officers to whom the management of the University press is intrusted : they meet in the parlour of the printing-office ; but cannot act unless five are present, one of whom must be the Vice-chancellor.

TARDY ; to be noticed for coming late into chapel. " I have known," says Gilbert Wakefield, " a sleepy devotee delayed so long by the drowsy God, as to make it requisite to come at last without his clothes ; and he has stood shivering with the flimsy fig-leaf of a surplice to veil his outward fellow."— *(Memoirs, p.* 147.)

Haply, some friend may shake his hoary head,
    And say—" Each morn, unchill'd by frosts, he ran
With hose ungarter'd, o'er yon turfy bed,
    To reach the chapel ere the psalms began"—

i. e. to escape being TARDY.

TAXORS, must be M. A.'s, and are Regents by virtue of their office. They are appointed to regulate the markets, examine the assize of bread, the lawfulness of weights and measures, and to call all the abuses and defects thereof into the Commissary's court.

TEN YEAR-MEN ; gentlemen who are admitted of any College, being twenty-four years of age and upwards, to take the degree of B. D. at the end of ten years. During the last two years, they must reside the greater part of three several terms.—Exercises the same as required for other Bachelors in Divinity.

TERM; there are three terms or periods of residence in each year, the major part of each of which the Student is obliged to *keep*; namely, the Michaelmas, Lent, and Easter terms. The first begins Oct. 10th, and ends 16th Dec. The second begins 13th of Jan. and its termination, as well as the commencement of the third, is regulated by the fall of Easter. The third ends on the Friday after commencement day (quod vide). For the terms necessary to be kept for the degree of B. A. See A. B.

The following lively imitation of Horace, Lib. i. Ode iv. on the commencement of Term, may not be unacceptable to our readers :—

> Vacation's o'er,—in every street
> We soon shall many a Cantab meet;
> For hither numbers daily hie,
> Or by the Tele,* or the Fly.*
> Once more the halls, so desert late,
> With smoking cheer, our senses greet;
> Freshmen and Sophs, with one intent,
> Haste to the scene of merriment.
> O'er *Alma Mater's* sacred head,
> Who widely late her banner spread,

* Two celebrated coaches.

Fell solitude,—to jocund song,
Now yields her reign, usurp'd too long:
While Bacchus, rosy god of wine !
And Venus, with her joys divine,
Dispute the Empire with the Nine.
But would you reach the heights of fame,
And glory from Apollo's claim ;
Now, now, the chaplet 'gin to weave,
Now, vows to favouring heaven give.
For Death, whose unrelenting hand,
No mortal prowess can withstand,
Strikes surely, with impartial dart,
Masters' and under-graduates' heart ;
And the short space that here we tarry,—
At least, " *in statu pupillari*,"
Forbids our growing hopes to germ,
Alas ! beyond the appointed term.
Nay, even now our time is o'er,
And January threatening lower,*
And warn us quickly to resign
The jovial monarchy of wine ;
To fresh-men yield the boasted claim,
As from the boards we take our name.

TERM-TROTTERS ; young men who contrive
to be *in* College the night before the division of the
term, and *out* of it the morning after the close.

TICK, a creditor.   To TICK ; to go on trust.

---

* The month in which the B. A. degree is taken, and which, in many instances, is the " finis fatorum ;" at least to a great portion of the "bons vi-
vans."

Tir'd at length with his tutor, and teas'd with his task,
    He silently raves round his desolate cavern,
'Till he *ticks* for another oblivious flask,
    And imports a fresh cargo of fun from the tavern.

                       Camb. Tart, 76.

So in Foote's Liar:

Old Wild. Now, Sir, it is incumbent on you to discharge your debt.

Young Wild. *In the College phrase*, I shall beg leave to TICK a little longer.

" It is a merry saying which they have at Oxford, when any tradesman is grown rich by trusting the Scholars, that his *faith* hath made him whole." *Terræ Filius*, No. 33. The following lines of Tom Randolph (a writer of great genius, whose works, however, have long ceased to be redde), are not destitute of *humour;* though TICKING, it must be allowed, is a very SERIOUS thing.

Hark, reader! if thou never yet hadst one,
I'll shew the torments of a CAMBRIDGE *dun*—
He rails where'er he comes, and yet can say
But this, that Randolph does not KEEP his day.
What! can I keep the *day*, or, stop the sun
From setting, or the night from coming on?

   -   -   -   -   -   -   -   -   -
   -   -   -   -   -   -   -   -

These evil spirits haunt me every day,
And will not let me study, eat, or pray.
I'm so much in their books, that, it is known,
I am too seldom frequent in my *own*.

What damage given to my doors might be,
If doors might actions have of BATTERY?
And when they find their coming to no end,
They dun by proxy, and their letters send,
In such a style as I could never find
In Tully's long, or Seneca's short wind.

"Good Master Randolph, pardon me, I pray,
If I *remember** you *forget* your day.
I kindly dealt with you, and it would be
Unkind in you not to be kind to me, &c.
Thus hoping you will make a courteous end,
I *rest*" (I WOULD THOU WOULDST!) your loving
friend, &c.   *Camb. Tart*, 10.

Of the origin, or etymology, of the term TICK, no conjecture has been offered. It seems to me to be a di-
minutive of TICKET, a check. This conjecture may
derive support from the following passage in Decker's
Gul's Hornbook, 1609. Speaking of the gallants who
go by water to the playhouse—' No matter upon
landing whether you have money, or no—You may
swim in twentie of their boats over the river upon
TICKET.'

THIRDING; ' a custom practised at the Universities, where two *thirds* of the original price is allowed by the Upholsterers to the Students for house-
hold goods returned them within the year.'—(*Grose's
Dict.*)

---

* To *remember* formerly signified to remind.

TRIPOS ; a long piece of white and brown paper, like that on which the commonest ballads are printed, containing Latin hexameter verses, with the list of the mathematical honours, with the author's name, &c. The Cambridge TRIPOS, it has been conjectured, was probably in old time delivered like the Terræ Filius from a *Tripod*, a three-legged stool, in humble imitation of the Delphic Oracle. It is mentioned in the statute de tollendis ineptiis in publicis disputationibus,* an. 1626————ut prævaricatores, *tripodes*, alii que omnes disputantes veterum academiæ formam, &c.

TRIPOS CLASSICAL, in conformity with regulations, confirmed by a Grace of the Senate, in 1822, a voluntary Classical examination of commencing Bachelors who have obtained *mathematical honours*, has been established, and a Classical Tripos will in future be published similar to the Mathematical one.

* The following, from the facetious Fuller, will serve to shew to what lengths they went formerly *in ineptiis* See his ' Worthies,' edit. 1684. ' When Morton, afterwards bishop of Durham, stood for the degree of D. D. at Cambridge, he advanced something which was displeasing to the Professor, who exclaimed, with some warmth, Commosti mihi *stomachum*. To whom Morton replied, Gratulor tibi, Reverende Professor, de bono tuo *stomacho*, cænabis apud me hâc nocte.' The *English* word *Stomach* formerly signified *passion, indignation*. Archbishop Cranmer appointed one *Travers* to a fellowship at Trinity College, who had been before rejected (says my author), on account of his *intolerable stomach*. This would be thought a singular discommendation in the present day.—To add another story from Fuller, relating PUBLICIS DISPUTATIONIBUS.

' When a professor of logic pressed an answerer, a better Christian than a Clerk, with a hard argument ; Reverende Professor (said he), ingenue confiteor me non posse respondere huic argumento. To whom the professor —*Recte respondes*.' (*Holy and Profane State*.)

TUITION. The quarterly payments of persons in statu pupillari, in every College, are the following:

	£.	s.	d.
Nobleman - - - - - -	10	0	0
Fellow-Commoner - - -	5	0	0
Pensioner - - - - - -	2	10	0
Sizar - - - - - - - -	0	15	0
B. A. Fellow-Commoner -	2	0	0
B. A. - - - - - - - -	1	0	0

UNDERGRADUATES. Students who have not yet taken a degree.

VACATION. There are three Vacations at Cambridge: the Christmas, Easter, and the Long Vacation; and it appears from the following extract, that however great the affection of Cantabs may be for their Alma Mater, still they leave her at these periods without much regret:

> Farewell, thou willow'd stream,
> Glittering bright with wisdom's beam,
> Silver Cam! whose bowers among
> Inspiration leads her throng;
> Clio breathes celestial fire;
> Music hangs her dulcet lyre:
> Yet farewell! to brighter joys
> Pleasure lifts her wandering eyes,
> With her own resistless smile
> She shall smooth each care awhile:
> Yes, she, fair queen, shall all the mind possess,
> With gladness fire it, and with rapture bless.
> *C. T. Hartis*, 1763.

VICE-CHANCELLOR. This Officer is annually elected, on the 4th of November, by the Senate. His

I

office, in the absence of the Chancellor, embraces the execution of the Chancellor's powers, and the Government of the University according to her Statutes. He must, by an Order made in 1587, be the Head of some College; and during his continuance in Office he acts as a Magistrate for the University and County. The Junior Master is generally nominated to this Office.

UNION. A celebrated Debating Society in Cambridge, composed entirely of Members of the University, where political subjects were discussed, which the Master of St. John's suppressed during his Vice-chancellorship, in 1817; on which occasion the following spirited Parody on the Bard, by the late M. Lawson, Esq. M. P. for Boroughbridge, and Fellow of Magdalen College, made its appearance:

I. 1.

' Ruin seize thee, senseless prig !
  ' Confusion on thy " optics" wait !
' Though prais'd by many a Johnian pig,
  ' They crowd the shop in fruitless state.
' Hood, nor Doctor's scarlet gown,
' Nor N—th, nor P—th shall win renown ;
' Nor save thy secret soul from nightly fears,
' The UNION'S curse, the UNION'S tears.
Such were the sounds that o'er the pedant pride
  Of W—d, the Johnian, scatter'd wild dismay,
As down the flags of Petty-Cury's* side
  He wound with toilsome march his long array,
Stout T–th–m stood aghast with puffy face,
" To arms !" cried Beverly,† and couch'd his qui-
    v'ring mace.

---

* The street in which the Society was held.
† One of the Esquire Bedells, who bear the mace.

I. 2.

At a window, which on high
　　Frowns o'er the market-place below,
With trowsers* on, and haggard eye,
　　A member stood immersed in woe.
His tatter'd gown, and greasy hair
Stream'd like a dishclout to the onion'd air,
And with a voice that well might beat the cryer,
Struck the deep sorrows of his lyre :—
' Hark ! how each butcher's stall, and mightier shop,
　' Sighs to the market's clattering row beneath;
' For thee the women squall, the cleavers chop,
　　' Revenge on thee in hoarser murmurs breathe.
' Vocal no more since Monday's fatal night
' To Thirlwall's† keen remark, or †Sheridan's wild
　　flight.

I. 3.

' Mute now is Raymond's† tongue,
　' That hushed the Club to sleep :
' The patriot Whitcombe† now has ceased to rail;
　' Waiters in vain ye weep.
' Lawson,† whose annual song
　' Made the Red Lion‡ wag his raptur'd tail.

---

　* The savage despair of the Member is finely pourtrayed by the trowsers.
A total indifference to moral guilt or personal danger is argued by his thus
appearing before the Vice-chancellor : that gentleman justly regarding the
wearing of trowsers as the most atrocious of moral offences, and having
lately deservedly excluded a distinguished Wrangler who had been guilty of
them, from a Fellowship of his College.

　" Crure tenus medio tunicas succingere debet."—*Juvenal, Sat. VI.* 445.

　Tempora mutantur. Trowsers are now universally and fearlessly sported
by men of every standing.
　† Speakers of the Society.
　‡ A magnificent, though bold figure. The Red Lion (which is the sign of

' Dear lost companions in the spouting art,
  ' Dear as the commons smoking in the hall,
' Dear as the Audit ale that warms my heart,—
  ' Ye fell amidst the dying Union's fall.

II. 1.

' Weave the warp, and weave the woof,
  ' The winding-sheet of J–mmy's race;
' Give ample room and verge enough
  ' To mark revenge, defeat, disgrace.
' Mark the month, and mark the day,
' The Senate widely echoing with the fray;
' Commoner, Sizar, Pensioner, and Snob,
' Shouts of an undergraduate mob.

II. 2.

' Master of a mighty College,
  ' Without his robes behold him stand,
' Whom not a Whig will now acknowledge,
  ' Return his bow, or shake his hand.
' Is the sable Jackson fled?
' Thy friend is gone—he hides his powder'd head.
' The Bedells, too, by whom the mace is borne?
' Gone to salute the rising morn.
' Fair laughs the morn, and soft the zephyr blows;
  ' While gently sidling through the crowded street,
' In scarlet robe, Clare's* tiny Master goes.
   ' Ware† clears the road, and Gunning† guides his
     feet,

the Inn at which the Union assembled), and which is a remarkably handsome lion of the kind, is described as wagging his tail, in testimony of the pleasure he felt at the goings on within.

    * The Vice-chancellor elect.
     † Two of the Esquire Bedells.

' Regardless of the sweeping whirlwind's sway,
' That, hush'd in grim repose, marks **J–mmy** for its
 prey.

II. 3.

' Fill high the Audit bowl!
 ' The feast in hall prepare!
' 'Reft of his robes, he yet may share the feast,
 ' Close by the Master's chair.
' Contempt and laughter scowl
' A baleful smile upon their baffled guest.—
 ' Heard ye the din of battle bray,
' Gown to gown, and cap to cap?
' Hark at the Johnian Gates each thund'ring rap,
 ' While thro' opposing Dons they move their way.
' Ye Johnian towers, old **W—d's** eternal shame,
 ' With many a midnight imposition fed,
' Revere his algebra's immortal fame,
 ' And spare the meek Mechanic's holy head.
' Each bristled *boar* will bear no more,
' And meeting in the Combination Room,
' They stamp their vengeance deep, and ratify his
 doom.

III. 1.

' **J–mmy**, lo! to sudden fate,
 (Pass the wine—the liquor's good)
' Half of thy year we consecrate:
 ' The web is now what was the *wood*.
' But mark the scene beneath the Senate's height—
 ' See the petition's crowded skirts unroll;
' Visions of glory spare my aching sight,
 ' Unborn commencements crowd not on my soul.

' No more our Kaye,* our Thackeray,* we bewail;
' All hail! thou genuine Prince,† Britannia's issue
    hail!

III. 2.

' Heads of houses, Doctors bold,
   ' Sublime their hoods and wigs they rear;
' Masters young, and Fellows old,
   ' In bombazeen and silk appear.
' In the midst a form divine,
' His eye proclaims him of the British line.
' What cheers of triumph thunder thro' the air,
   ' While the full tide of youthful thanks is pour'd!
' Hear from your chambers, Price‡ and Hibbert,‡ hear;
   ' Th' oppressor shrinks, the Union is restor'd.
' The treasurer flies to spread the news he brings,
' And wears, for triumph's sake, yet larger chitter-
    lings.

III. 3.

' Fond, impious man, think'st thou thy puny fist,
   ' Thy " *Wood*-en Sword" has broke a British club?
' The Treasurer soon augments our growing list,—
   ' We rise more numerous from this transient rub.
' Enough for me : with joy I see
   ' The different doom our fates assign ;
' Be thine contempt and big-wigged care,
   ' To triumph, and to die, are mine.'
He spoke, and headlong from the window's height,
Deep in a dung-cart near, he plung'd to endless night.

    This Society is now happily restored, and is sup-

---

* Former Vice-chancellors.   † The Chancellor.
       ‡ Speakers of the Society.

ported by men of every standing. The Debates, however, are restricted to events previous to 1800: and no new subject is allowed to be introduced after 10 o'clock.

WOODEN SPOON, for wooden heads: the last* of those candidates for the degree of A.B. who take honours: the lowest of the Junior Optime's. After *woooden spoon,* follow the οι πολλοι. It is an old saying, that, *Wranglers* are born with *golden* spoons in their mouths, Senior Optime's with *silver,* Junior Optime's with wooden, and the οι πολλοι with *leaden* ones! "What is heavier than *lead?* and what is the name thereof, but a fool?"—(*Ecclus. XXII.* 14.)

WRANGLER,—(Senior Wrangler.) The highest honour in the Schools.

' When sage Mathesis calls her Sons to fame,
' The *Senior Wrangler* bears the highest name.'

" The ancients," says a learned lady, " left our cotemporaries little to improve upon even in this art (Wrangling); and Hume is not a neater Sophist than Protagoras; who, in a controversy between himself and his disciple, baffled the Judges, as old story tells, with a dilemma not ill worth repeating. A rich

---

* Who while he lives, must wield the boasted prize,
   Whose value all can feel, the weak, the wise;
   Displays in triumph his distinguish'd boon,
   The solid honours of the wooden spoon.

                                   (Vide Camb. Tart. 98.)

Quere. Ought not the *Junior Optime's* to be arranged alphabetically? Not that we had the honour of being ξυλοφοροι, or bearers of the wooden Standard.

young man, EVATHLUS by name, desired to learn his method of puzzling causes; and paying him half the sum agreed upon at first, promised him the other half when he should have gained his first cause. When the time of study was past, Evathlus, called away to some other employment, forbore pleading in the courts; and Protagoras, weary of waiting, sued him for the money, urging this, as he hoped, unanswerable argument:—' Either I gain my cause, and you, Evathlus, will be condemned to pay; or you, having gained it, will be obliged to pay according to the original terms of our agreement.' But the young man having learned to WRANGLE as well as his master, soon retorted upon him the following dilemma:— ' Either the judges discharge me, and of course the debt is made void; or they condemn me, by which event I equally save my money: for being condemned to lose, I have clearly not gained my first cause.'

" 'Tis said that the matter remained ever undecided: yet from this, *perhaps*, the young men *obtaining the first mathematical honours at Cambridge are termed* WRANGLERS."—*(Piozzi's British Synonym. Vol. II.)*

YEOMAN BEDELL. This officer's chief duty is to attend the Commissary on all occasions of holding his Courts. He is appointed by letters patent, under the hand and seal of the Chancellor.

'JEMMY GORDON.'

" Who to save from *Rustication*,
" *Crams* the dunce with declamation! "

READING AND VARMINT

METHOD OF PROCEEDING

TO THE

DEGREE OF BACHELOR OF ARTS:

BEING A TAIL-PIECE TO THE

GRADUS AD CANTABRIGIAM;

OR,

NEW UNIVERSITY GUIDE.

THE Freshman who is ignorant of the course of study he is to pursue at the University, will find ample information in the pages of the CAMBRIDGE CALENDAR; but as he cannot be expected to devote every hour of his undergraduateship to reading, he must find out amusements for his leisure moments, and a few agreeable friends to be the companions of his mirth, and his exercises, as well as his studies. To obtain companions, he must be inducted, and to pass his leisure time in conviviality and mirth, he must give or be invited to entertainments. At these entertainments he will meet with other PROMISING young men of various descriptions, and he will naturally be inducted to, and make acquaintances amongst, a portion of these young men. Now it is undeniable that a young man for his improvement, mental as well as coporeal, must see society; and he will naturally copy the manners of his College acquaintances, in order that he might not seem a different being amongst them. He will enter into their pursuits, do the same as they do, and, in short, proceed to the degree of B. A. in the regular *varmint* manner.

Now the *varmint* way to proceed to B. A. degree is this—Cut Lectures, go to Chapel as little as possible, dine in hall seldom more than once a week, give *Gaudies* and *Spreads*, keep a horse or two, go to NEWMARKET, attend the six-mile bottom, drive a drag, wear *varmint* clothes and well-built coats, be up to smoke, a rum one at Barnwell,* a regular go at New Zealand,* a staunch admirer of the bottle, and care a damn for no man. "At lucre or renown let others aim," for a *varmint*-man spurns a scholarship, would consider it a degradation to be a fellow; and as for taking an *honour*, it would be about the very last idea that could enter his head. What cares he for Tutors or Proctors, for Masters or Vice-chancellors, since his whole aim is pleasure and amusement, since a day's hard reading would drive him half mad or give him the blue devils; since subordination is a word of the meaning of which he professes to be ignorant; and since rows and sprees are the delight of his soul. He is never seen in academicals till hall time, or towards evening, and then only puts them on for "*dacency's sake*," or because it is a custom throughout the "*varsity*." But in the day, he is seen in a *Jarvey* tile, or a low-crowned-broad-brim, a pair of white swell tops, *varmint* inexpressibles, a regular flash waistcoat, and his coat of a nameless cut; his "*cloth*" of the most uncommon pattern, tied after his own way, and a short crookt-stick or bit o' plant in his hand; and thus he goes out riding : or he may dress differently, and lounge through the streets, always in company with a friend or two, visiting saddlers, milliners, barbers, bootmakers, and tailors; or looking in

---

* Celebrated as the residences of the Cyprian tribes.

at a friend's rooms, and to arrange matters for the day: or, if fine, he may make up a water-party, if in the summer term, and go down the CAMUS in a six-oar, dine at Clay-hive, or Ditton, or take a snack at Chesterton, and return in the evening; or he may walk out to Chesterton to play at billiards, and return *plus* or *minus* the sum he started with ; or he may drive out in a buggy; or do fifty other things, and enter into fifty other schemes, all productive of amusement. In the evening he dines at his own rooms, or at those of a friend, and afterwards blows a cloud, puffs at a segar, and drinks copiously. He then sings a song, tells a story, comments on the events of the day, talks of horses, gives his opinion on the ensuing race between Highflyer and Emilius, or makes bets on the late fight between *Spring* and *Langan.* After this the whole party sit down to unlimited loo, and half-guinea, or guinea points, and here again he comes off *plus* or *minus* £40 or £50. If he has lost, he is no way concerned at it, for he is sure of winning as much the succeeding night; he therefore takes his glass or sits down to supper, and gets to bed about two or three in the morning. Determined to *sleep a few,* and after having cast off his habiliments, he hops into bed, and snores—somno vinoque gravatus, till about six in the evening, and then gets up more sleepy than ever. He dresses; but having no appetite, eats nothing, drinks a glass of soda-water, and walks to a friend's rooms, where he relates his adventures and excites the risibility of his auditors. He then resolves on a ride, and without togging for the occasion, just puts on his tile and mounts his prad. Determining to be very steady and sober for the future, i. e. for the next twelve hours, he urges his steed along the Trumpington Road, goes

out by the Shelford Common, and returns home between eight and nine. He then feels as if he could eat
something, and accordingly he does, by way of supper, and retires to his rooms, with an intention of
being quiet, and in order to go early to bed. But lo!
he is told by his *Gyp* that the Master or Dean has
sent a message desiring to see him the next morning.
Well knowing what this is for, he *goeth* to bed and
cons over in his own mind what to say in extenuation
of his irregularities, and so *falleth* to sleep. Next
day, he calls at the appointed time, when the M. C.
with a countenance not to be surpassed in gravity,
informs him for the last week he has been very irregu-
lar, and requires an account of the circumstances
which occasioned the said irregularity. For the
gate-bill thus standeth: Monday night, out till 3
o'clock; Tuesday ½ past 4; Wednesday ½ past 2;
Thursday ¼ past 3; Friday ½ past 4; Saturday—
all night. His excuses are that he has been at
different parties, where he was detained late, and
where he has found the society so agreeable, and the
time fly so imperceptibly fast, that morning has broke
in upon him ere he imagined it was an hour past midnight. This draws down a very heavy invective
against parties altogether, and a still longer and more
tedious lecture on the dangerous tendency of such
conduct, so directly opposite to the laws and discipline of the University; and a conclusive paragraph
containing (amongst other things) a pardon for past
offences, but with an assurance that a repetition
of similar conduct cannot but meet with a concomi-
tant cheque in proportion to its enormity, in either
rustication or expulsion. Thus dismissed the august
presence, he recounts this jobation to his friends, and
enters into a discourse on masters, deans, tutors, and

proctors, and votes chapel a *bore*, and *gates* a complete nuisance. But is this all? No. He has resolved to treat *the dons* with contempt, and go on more gaily than ever. Accordingly he cuts chapel, and issues forth at night *sine* cap and gown, with a segar in his mouth. He is determined to have a lark with two or three more, and away they go. While they are pulling the girls about in the streets, up comes the Proctor: " Pray, Sir, may I ask if you are a member of the University ?"—" Yes, Sir, I am."—" Your name and college, Sir, if you please." It is given without the least hesitation. The next morning a *bull-dog* calls on Mr. Varmint, to deliver a message from the Proctor, viz:—That he is fined 6s. 8d. for being in the streets without his cap and gown, and that he would be glad to see him at 12 o'clock that day. Now he has to call on the Proctor, and in he goes with a very surly countenance. The Proctor puts on one of his most severe phizzes, and informs him that his conduct in the streets'last night was most ungentlemanlike and improper, against every rule of order and propriety, and in open opposition to the Academic discipline, and contempt of him and his office. That such conduct deserved much severer chastisement than he was willing to inflict, but that he should be neglecting the duty he owed to his office and the University if he overlooked it. He therefore desires him to get three hundred verses of Homer's Iliad, Book 2d. by heart, and requests he will by no means leave the University until it was said. After a great deal of opposition, excuses, and protestations, he finds himself not a bit better off, for the Proctor will not mitigate a syllable, and he is obliged to stomach the *impos.* and retire. For the first hour or two afterwards he makes

himself very uneasy about this, but he at length resolves not to learn it, whatever should be the consequence. He therefore goes out to a party, makes
himself very merry, and cares not a fig about the
matter. Next morning he happens, unlucky wight!
to meet with the Dean, who accosts him, " Pray,
Mr. Varmint, why have you not been to Chapel
lately ? I have very seriously to complain of your
non-attendance. You have not attended for nearly a
fortnight, excepting Sundays, and you cannot expect
that I, or any man, in the capacity I hold, can
overlook such gross irregularity. However, you may
think what you like, but I am determined to do my
duty towards the College, and to see that you attend
regularly. But as that has by no means been the
case, and as you have so disrespectfully absented
yourself, I really must take notice of it in a severe
way. I am very sorry for it, nobody more so, but it
is an imperative duty I must fulfil. You will get by
heart 500 lines of Virgil, the 7th Æneid, and I expect
it will be said with alacrity and promptitude. Good
morning, Sir." So here is Mr. Varmint with two
impositions *in hand* which must be very soon *in head:*
one, if not said, will beget rustication, and the other,
if neglected, will cause the Dean to tell him to take
his name off the boards of the College. He debates
in his own mind as to whether it is better to get them
or not; but at length determines to see Proctors,
Deans, and in short the whole University at Old Nick,
rather than look at a word; and

" —to take arms against a sea of troubles,
" And, by opposing, end them."

Alas! how soon do mortals change their firmest
and most fixed resolutions! How many circum-

stances occur to induce them to act contrary to their resolves. Mr. Varmint, by drinking too much wine for the last two days, rather prematurely finds himself very much the worse from his late Cyprian adventures, and in fact is compelled to send for a surgeon. In short, Varmint is obliged to get an *ægrotat*, to confine himself to his rooms, and lie still on the sofa. On his table are draughts, powders, and lotions; the surgeon visits him daily. What is he to do all day by himself on the sofa? His friends are with him a great deal to drive away melancholy; but still he has an immensity of leisure time on his hands. He must read; but what? Walter Scott? No, he hates novels, and all that kind of trash. Lord Byron? He has read him fifty times, and he wants something new. He thought of every thing; but at last resolved to spend his time in learning the three hundred lines of Greek, and the five hundred lines of Virgil, for the Proctor and Mr. Dean. In the mean time the term divides; and his companions, or the majority of them, leave the University for their several homes. He, of course, wishes to leave likewise; but he is ill, and cannot depart before he is better, which the surgeon does not choose should be the case for some time; and even if he were well, he could not go before the Dean signed his " *exeat*," which he would not do before the imposition was said; so he is hemmed in on all sides, and has the blue devils, besides a prospect of growing hippish. He, therefore, spends the time he would have passed in pleasure at home, in the shady court of a college, and stuffs himself with Greek and Latin hexameters, and lives entirely on barley-water and medicine, for the space of three weeks. At the end of this time, we will suppose him getting again convalescent, and recovering his wonted spirits. He satisfies the Proctor and the Dean by saying a part of each *impos.*, and after bitterly cursing the place, leaves it for the country. This is the way that many men spend their three years at the University. But, Mr. Freshman, whoever you may be, I write this for your especial benefit, and leave it to yourself to copy or avoid such conduct, as you may think proper.

After the long vacation, Mr. Varmint comes up again to reside. His sprees of his first year, and their consequences, have gained him experience, and he knows how to manage in a scientific way. To avoid gate-bills, he will be out at night as late as he pleases, and will defy any one to discover his absence; for he will climb over the College walls, and fee his Gyp well, when he is out all night. To avoid impositions from the Dean, he will attend more regularly at Chapel; which, though a great bore, must yet be endured : and to get clear from the clutches of the Proctors, he will scud when there is need ; and if followed, will floor the *bull-dogs*, and bolt. He now is twice as gay as before, rides, courses, hunts, shoots, fishes, drives, drinks, fights, swears, rows, and gambles, more than ever. He dresses still more like an eccentric fancy man, and acts yet more unlike what he ought to do, and thus he passes his terms. But now comes the time when he is to be examined for the *Little-go;* and about three weeks before the examination he begins to read. He finds himself unequal to the task, without *cramming.* He in consequence engages a private tutor, and buys all the cram-books published for the occasion. After reading himself ill, he goes in; and by the greatest luck

in the world, happens to pass. This puts him in high
spirits again, and he gives a large *Spread,* and gets
drunk on the strength of it. He continues to have a
private tutor for the remainder of his residence, and
reads with him about one day in a term, until the last
term in his third year, when he is obliged to read for
his degree of *Bachelor of Arts.* Accustomed to mirth
and gaiety, and to all kinds of sporting pursuits, never
having opened a single mathematical book since his
residence, knowing Euclid only by name, and Algebra
still less, if possible; not being a dab at Latin or
Greek; in short, never having professed to be a reading man, Mr. Varmint begins to encounter all the
difficulties attending on such a career, when near its
termination in severe study. He has now recourse
to his private tutor, who finds him miserably defi-
cient; and to work they both go, the one cramming,
and the other unable to swallow a mouthful. He falls
ill by reading hard, being so unused to it, and gives
it up for a week, then sets to again, and so goes on till
the day of examination, when he may perhaps muster
up resolution enough to go into the *Senate-house.* If
he does go in, and is well enough crammed, he gets
a station amongst the apostles; if not, he may per-
chance be plucked. But if he does not think he shall
be able to go through, he reads on a little longer, and
goes out at a *bye-term.* This is his career at college;
what it may be in after-life, is quite another affair.
When he has got his degree in either of these ways,
with the rest of his companions, he sits down with all
of them, about forty or fifty, to a most *glorious spread,*
ordered from the college cook, to be served up in the
most swell style possible. They are about two hours

and a half at dinner; and afterwards set to, and get most awfully drunk, each man having floored upwards of three bottles of port, independent of champagne and madeira at dinner, or burgundy and claret. Thus they conclude the last feast they shall ever have together at College, and another fortnight sees them all, perhaps, wafted far from the University, some of them for ever.

" Farewell to the towers! Farewell to the bowers!
  Where the sage wizard ART all his charms hath
        display'd;
And sweet science cowers, amongst blooming flowers,
  In gay robes of glory majestic array'd.

Farewell, banks of Camus! thou fair scenes of blisses,
  The Muse, Love's, and Graces' invincible seat!
Your silver soft stream, like the tide of Illyssus,
  Aye, fresher than airs of Hygeia's retreat.

Ye cloisters low bending, and proudly extending,
  To cherish young Genius and Taste in your gloom;
The spirit befriending, as softly descending,
  It mounts in pure incense to Heav'n's vaulted doom.

From you I must sever; then farewell for ever
  Each heart-honour'd object that swells my last
        theme;
The world is a field I must enter, but never
  Can ought charm my soul like your shadeACADEME!
                              (*Camb. Tart*, 271.)

This is *one way* of proceeding to the degree of B. A. The " reading man" goes to work in quite another style. He attends lectures regularly, never misses chapel, dines nearly always in hall, takes moderate exercise, is rarely out of College after the gates are shut, reads twelve hours a day, strives hard to get prizes and medals, always obtains a scholarship, seldom gets " a little the worse for liquor," gives no swell parties, runs very little into debt, takes his cup of bitch at night, and goes quietly to bed, and thus he passes his time in a way a Varmint man would despise. These are the men who run off with all the prizes and obtain wranglers' degrees, who get made fellows and tutors, and who become eventually the principal men in the University. But these are by no means the most gifted men, the men of the most brilliant talent, or greatest genius. But they are the *steady* men, who owe all their knowledge to hard reading, and desperate perseverance in study. Of course there are many—very many exceptions; but what I state is for the most part the case. I conclude this account by stating, that many things in it are extenuated, but " nought set down in malice;" and the observant student of a twelvemonth's standing in the University, if his acquaintance is at all extensive, will find the truth of my assertions. This is written by one who has witnessed scenes such as he has herein glanced at, and who thinks it will be an excellent *Tail-piece* to the GRADUS AD CANTABRIGIAM; or, NEW UNIVERSITY GUIDE.

FINIS.

Printed by J. F. DOVE, St. John's Square.

Printed in the United States
By Bookmasters